T0113664

UNEARTH
YOUR INTUITION

UpLevel and Transform Your Life
Using Your Inner Superpowers

JENNIFER S. ABRA

BALBOA.PRESS
A DIVISION OF HAY HOUSE

Copyright © 2020 Jennifer S. Abra.

All rights reserved. No part of this book may be used or reproduced by any means, graphic, electronic, or mechanical, including photocopying, recording, taping or by any information storage retrieval system without the written permission of the author except in the case of brief quotations embodied in critical articles and reviews.

Balboa Press books may be ordered through booksellers or by contacting:

Balboa Press
A Division of Hay House
1663 Liberty Drive
Bloomington, IN 47403
www.balboapress.com
844-682-1282

Because of the dynamic nature of the Internet, any web addresses or links contained in this book may have changed since publication and may no longer be valid. The views expressed in this work are solely those of the author and do not necessarily reflect the views of the publisher, and the publisher hereby disclaims any responsibility for them.

The author of this book does not dispense medical advice or prescribe the use of any technique as a form of treatment for physical, emotional, or medical problems without the advice of a physician, either directly or indirectly. The intent of the author is only to offer information of a general nature to help you in your quest for emotional and spiritual well-being. In the event you use any of the information in this book for yourself, which is your constitutional right, the author and the publisher assume no responsibility for your actions.

Any people depicted in stock imagery provided by Getty Images are models, and such images are being used for illustrative purposes only.
Certain stock imagery © Getty Images.

Print information available on the last page.

ISBN: 978-1-9822-5298-4 (sc)
ISBN: 978-1-9822-5299-1 (e)

Balboa Press rev. date: 08/21/2020

CONTENTS

ACKNOWLEDGMENTS

I would first like to thank my Mentors, ***Heather***, for teaching me all about the Spirit world and most importantly how to meditate. Without your guidance, I would never have learned how to connect with Spirit, conduct readings accurately or have found the drive to pursue my new-found passion of mediumship.

I would also like to thank ***my very first Unearth Your Intuition students*** who trusted me to be their first teacher on their journey. You guys were the best guinea pigs a girl could ever ask for. I hope you are still doing your meditations!

To ***my family***, for first thinking I was crazy for quitting my teaching job with the school board to speak to the invisible and for supporting my decision anyway because you love me. Your faith in me moves mountains and keeps me going, even when I want to quit. To ***Chad*** for supporting me once again when I decided last minute to run off to Costa Rica to finish this book because my soul said to do it.

Thank you to ***Jenn*** with two "n's" for inviting me to your condo near the beach and for helping kick my behind into gear.

Thank you to ***Nikolina Zelic*** for always intuitively capturing my essence in your beautiful photo art.

www.maidentomotherphotoart.com

Visit The Creative Zoo on Facebook
www.facebook.com/thecreativezoo.ca

Thank you to ***Raymond Aaron*** for this amazing opportunity to publish my very first book.

DEDICATED TO MY CLIENTS AND STUDENTS OF UNEARTH YOUR INTUITION

This book is dedicated to all of my Unearth Your Intuition students. You have validated and taken steps to discover that Spirit truly does exist and that there is more to this life than what you can see with your eyes. You have reflected to me repeatedly that a "skeptic" or non-believer in the power of connection can in fact transform lives. Your trust in me and Spirit is incredible. Thank you for allowing me to guide you in this ground-breaking program and for choosing me to be the one who helps you remember your true power. I saw your light when you didn't see it for yourself.

I also want to dedicate this book to all of my Mediumship clients. The ones who showed up at my door in tears from overwhelming grief, and the ones who crossed their arms and said, "I don't believe you." You both have taught me to believe in myself and in Spirit one hundred percent. I am truly honored to be a part of your grieving journey and my wish for you all is that you are that you find peace in your loss. That when you receive that dime, feather, bird, or song on the radio that you now KNOW that is a gift from them.

It is also dedicated to my son who threw the box of Lego. I'll explain later.

INTRODUCTION

Welcome to my book. A manifestation of mine, if you will. If you had told me ten, or even five years ago that I would be writing a book on intuition, I would have said you were crazy. What did I know about the subject of intuition? Not much. The information I was "remembering" at the time would have fit nicely onto a 3 x 5 index card or even one of those fluorescent sticky notes. Being a Mom of four young kids doesn't exactly allow us to pursue our destiny's. Instead it allows us to wipe noses and pack our diaper bags with baby items; not knowledge. I didn't write this book just for Moms, although I am positive it will resonate with you, especially if your kids are young like mine were back then. I didn't notice signs or repeating numbers. I was too focused on just surviving the day, as some of you are doing now. Just getting through it. Was it bed time yet? Mine or theirs.

I struggled a lot with depression in those early years. It used to feel like darkness was all around me, even on the sunniest of days. I was immersed in the Mom-ness and was not interested in being aware of MORE than that. I was a Mom and I had subconsciously decided that was my purpose in this lifetime. I loved my kids fiercely, but I had forgotten to return that love to myself.

Somehow, little by little, the journey would take a sharp right turn and everything I had known as reality was about to blow out of the water. As if the univers had taken my path into its own massive energetic hands and flipped my life upside down in a matter of seconds. All it took was a box of Legos.

I remember that moment in time that box flew across the air in my living room in April 2011. It was like the movie of my life was playing in slow motion on the screen. I had just cleaned the entire house (Why? I have four kids and it's like shoveling the walk in the middle of a snowstorm). My then 6- year-old was having a fit and took his 1000 pieces in that box and flung its contents across the entire span of the room. Sounds like a regular day, doesn't it? But that was THE moment. That pivotal moment in one's own life where literally everything changes. I guess the universe has a sense of humour deciding to use a toy to get my attention.

It was in that seemingly insignificant space in time that my entire insides shifted. My brain, my soul and my heart completely unraveled. I realized with a jolt that I didn't know who I was any longer and that I had somehow morphed into "just a Mom." No longer Jen, no longer a person, no longer willing to sacrifice my happiness or my warm dinners for tiny bodies again. The "snap" inside may have even been audible from the stained-couch if it hadn't been so loud from all the screaming my kids were doing.

That moment changed me forever. First for the absolute worst and then eventually for the best possible way imaginable. I just didn't see this side of it yet. Sometimes things must be destroyed so they can rise and be whole once more in a much more incredible way.

Two years later, I found myself on the floor in a heap. I didn't recognize my life or my body. I wanted to be done with everything, including life. As I sat on the floor sobbing uncontrollably and grieving who I had become, I was left with nothing. The choices I had made over the past two years of my life had left me helpless and desperate. That's when I heard "the voice" for the first time. The voice from above and to the right said in a very clear way, "Get off the floor. You have more to do." Am I going crazy? Who said that? It was enough to get me off the floor and into the shower. Where did this voice come from? I knew in an instant that it was a power much larger than myself. Even though I had no previous spiritual experience, I felt different somehow. Hopeful.

Things continued their path and I found myself wanting to learn and absorb everything I could get my hands on the topic of spirituality. Books began to literally fall off the shelves before my eyes. Crows began to follow me wherever I went. I was beginning to trust my intuition and follow those nudges. Those intuitive nudges and soft inner voices began to get louder every day and I listened. I had discovered my inner GPS without even knowing I had it.

I followed the breadcrumbs to various metaphysical stores, spiritual events, group meditations and Reiki. I loved the way it felt to hear the guidance and then follow it. I doubted sometimes being a newbie to this world, but I wanted more. I craved alone time. I meditated. I took a course on psychic development in the fall of 2013 which changed the game for me on an intuitive level. I began to see in my mind's eye visions and images that would ultimately manifest within hours or weeks. I predicted my van breaking down the morning of as a vision of a tow truck hook flashed before my eyes. Later that day, I found myself stranded on the side of the highway waiting for the tow truck to rescue me.

So many things began happening for me. The more I meditated, the stronger my intuition and gifts grew. Opportunities magically appeared for me. Doors opened and the more I followed it, the better my life became. I learned how to manifest and with practice, I got really good. Sometimes the things I asked for appear instantly. At the present time, I am writing this introduction in a tropical location that I also manifested. That Mom on the couch would never have imagined or wanted to take a trip across the world by herself. It wouldn't have seemed possible. And now because of my spiritual practice and following my intuition, I am here. Five years later.

Which brings me to this book.

Now that I have a strong spiritual knowing and have become a Mentor myself, I want to share with you all that I have "remembered" along the way. I didn't know I had this superpower back then. Maybe you don't know you have it either. Maybe you are lost in your own Mom-ness or maybe you are already on your journey. Either way, this book will help you in some capacity. For some, it will completely shift your beliefs and transform the way you think. For others, it will be validation that they are not "going crazy" but in fact are using their gifts already. Maybe you are a Lightworker and already know all this information but are ready to step into your light fully now because it encouraged you to step out of the spiritual closet. Who knows. All I do know is that you bought this book for a reason. If someone lent a copy to you, it's because you were meant to read it. If it fell off a shelf in front of you, you followed your intuition and picked it up. Congratulations. That was the first step on your journey with me.

Wherever you are on your path, I hope you know how amazing you are for pursuing your soul. Your soul knows the way. If you would just listen and trust a bit more, the possibilities are unlimited. When you are done this book, I hope you realize how powerful your thoughts and spoken words are. I hope you will know that the universe loves you so much that it led you here. To more knowledge, more manifesting and more magic.

I want to say thank you for trusting me to guide you to the magic. To your superpowers. Get ready to Unearth Your Intuition.

CHAPTER ONE

INTUITION

"The real truths of life are never entirely new to you because there is a level deep down within you where you already know the all the things, all those spiritual truths that you read or hear and then recognize them. Ultimately, it's not new information.
-Eckhart Tolle

AND WHEN I say, baby, I mean baby of the newborn kind. When you were born, you innately came to this Earth FULL of this inner knowledge. It has been there since you wore diapers and before you learned to crawl.

Think of how a newborn placed on their Mother's chest after birth, instinctively moves to nurse. How do they know what to do? We didn't give them an instruction manual, even though we totally wish they had come with one for us. We didn't teach them let alone shake their hand and say, "Hi, I'm your Mom. Nice to meet you. You're pretty cute. I think I'll keep you." Right? Babies just know stuff. They are full of this inner knowing. They were born with the gift of intuition.

The truth is we never lose this gift. Most of us grow up using it at minimum ability. When you were school-aged, you knew whether you wanted to be that kid's friend. You had a feeling you lost your homework. (Ok fine, maybe the dog ate it.) Then when you got a bit older and learned to drive your parent's car, you used it to navigate to your destination (I think we turn this way to Suzie's empty house where there are no parents and we are SO not going to drink.) Or whether someone we just met was good news or not.

As adults, we use those gut feelings a bit more while navigating the dating world. What feeling do you get when you meet someone new? Gut feelings help you decide if the guy you met is a total stalker or Prince Charming. The fact of the matter is it's there. It was there when you arrived in that hospital delivery room screaming your head off and it'll be there when you're old and grey in the nursing home, or your kid's house where you let THEM take care of you for a change.

It's IN you. Mostly being used for smallish things and basic survival needs. It resides within and because you picked up this book, you already know there is more to it. You sensed that you needed this book which means you must be ready to learn how to rock intuition's socks off. Superheroes wear capes, so they must wear socks.

Don't worry if you think you can't find your superpower just yet. It's there. And it's been there your whole life! Depending on how old you are, that's a long time. It's not going anywhere anytime soon.

You have a gift to share with the world. It would be a shame to keep it hidden.

And think you've only been giving it out in small quarters, like the birthday cake stuffed with money my grandma used to make us. No way. Quarters are for babies. Well, ok not baby babies. They might choke. Do not give that baby a quarter. But you know what I mean. If you dig into that delicious, money stuffed (chocolate?) cake, you can dig out maybe a ten and if your grandmother was generous, you can pull out a twenty.

Discovering your superpowers is one thing. Knowing you have them is something. It's what you do with the big stuff that therein the power lies. It's something we take for granted yet have so much of it to give. Right now, you've got quarters. Now how about we go for gold (or twenties in cold hard cash) and give this away. You will notice that you have survived on quarters since you came here.

Once you have finished this book, you will immediately see the difference within you if you put in the work. You have the ability, remember? Your soul has all the tools to set your life on fire if you'll just get out of your own damn way. Allow that inner knowing to bust out of the ordinary, boring, small quarters and upgrade it to incredible, life-altering abundance and power.

You've had the power all along, my dear. It's there waiting to be unearthed.

So, what exactly is intuition? Intuition is the inner knowing that you have inside of you. It's that gut feeling. The way you know which way to go, how you make decisions, and basically the way you survive. Without it we would all be completely and utterly lost. Literally. I like to call it a GPS system built inside of you. It's the tool we use to make both the important and the small decisions. Think of it as tool.

The issue is not whether we have it, because everyone does. The reason I'm writing this book is to show you how to use it on a much bigger scale for more than just surviving and decision-making. It's so much more than that. Through this book, I will show you how to dust off the rusty tool that has been sitting in the garden shed for many years. It's like the battery has drained. We're about to recharge it. Wait, scratch that. We're going to supercharge it. We'll bring it back to life and use it to create the most mind-blowing thing you've ever seen—your life. Together we're about to ramp it up, charge it to full battery, and use your intuition to its fullest potential.

I don't know why I used a boy example of a tool. It's just what my intuition said to write. And yes, you can use your intuition to write. I'm using it right now. I used my intuition to decide what the title of the book should be. I used it to decide who I was going to ask for help in publishing his book. I used it to decide whether to go to the event that brought the amazing people into my life helping me with this book. I could have ignored my intuition. I could have stayed home. But I didn't.

My gut told me to get in the car and drive on the busy highway (which I don't like to drive on), park my car in that creepy parking garage (which I'm terrified of), and walk into a place where I knew no one for an event that would change my life. Because my gut told me to do so. And it totally paid off. Do you see how that works now?

If I hadn’t used my intuition to find my way to the event and not trusted my gut to walk in and put on a brave face, my words wouldn't be here right now in your hands. Trust me, this is an awesome book and you will want to read all of it, especially if you want to do incredible things. Besides, you spent money on it and I don’t want you to waste your money. Money is the best.

I want you to start thinking of your intuition as a superpower, because that is exactly what it is. It is the motherlode of all super powers. It's like your Spidey senses on steroids. Eventually, (hopefully) you're going to wear it proudly. You’ll be like Clark Kent before he stepped into the phone booth with his nerd glasses and a slicked-back hair. Don't get me wrong he was cute. And so are you. I think. I can’t see you but I'm going to trust that you're cute. What I'm trying to say is that you have a superpower hidden underneath your work clothes. But instead of the “S” you have a big “I” on your chest. The thing is though, we all keep it hidden. Why are you hiding?

You can just keep your nerd glasses on, slick back your hair, and just keep your normal day-to- day job working at the Daily Planet without ever using your superpowers at all. OR You can step into the phone booth and come out with your amazing abilities. The choice is yours. Which sounds more appealing? If you ask me, I'd say get in that phone booth. And yes, I'm referencing 1980's retro movies. That's because I'm oldish. And I always like to talk about all things 80s and 90s. So, if you don't understand my Superman phone booth reference because you're in your twenties, don't worry, you can Google.

Once I Unearth it, then what?

At this point, I'm going to assume that you decided to take off the nerd glasses and show up with the cape. I feel kind of bad telling you that you had nerd glasses. But if you Google Superman 1970 then you'll understand. (What's up with all the boy references?) I'm just going to go with it because my intuition tells me so. Okay so, capes on. Big "I" on your chest, check. Now we're ready to fly.

Good choice. Now what That is an excellent question. Where do you begin? Your life is about to get ramped up. But the important thing is that you'll notice things are going to change slowly at first. Baby steps. Start small and work your way up the ladder.

Once you begin to unearth your intuition, you will be able to do the following things (if you decide they are what you're after):

- Your third eye will be WIDE open. This allows for your psychic/intuitive powers to expand and "see" or predict more and with more clarity. (More on this in the next chapter on Meditation.)
- You'll be more aware of the signs that are around you constantly.

- Messages from Source will be more abundant and noticeable.
- You can tune in to the high frequencies that help you co-create your entire life. Don't like where you are now? YOU have the power to change it.
- Once you tune-in and practice these new- found abilities, you will be able to intuitively "read" Angel Cards for yourself and then others.
- Your intuition and gut-feelings will become much stronger and you will be able to trust them more, thus making decisions much more quickly.
- You will establish a solid meditation routine that will last the rest of your life.
- Eventually, with a strong meditation practice, you can access and deliver messages from the other side (Become a Medium, like me!)
- There is more, but I don't want to freak you out. Yet.

I Like My Normal Life

Who doesn't love comfortable and normal? The life you've lived up until this point most likely sounded a lot like mine did.

If you had met me ten years ago, you wouldn't have thought to yourself, "Wow, one day that gal is going to talk to dead people!" No way! At the time, I was a new Mom with three small children and my days consisted of changing diapers and making sure I had a clean-ish shirt to wear out in public. I only concentrated on my family, maintaining my small townhome that was growing too small for my family and my career as a teacher at a small private school. Becoming a Medium was a course of action I had never in my wildest dreams imagined for myself, yet it was one of the best decisions I have ever made.

I even knew there was a spirit world. Books by John Edward and Sylvia Browne touched my dusty bookshelves for a short time, but my lifestyle didn't exactly support pursuing those matters more than that. There wasn't time, really. Live wasn't about me back then. My interests took a backseat to any remote possibility of pursuing anything other than what was in front of me. I saw only runny noses and a floor full of toys. Sound familiar?

Back then, I couldn't have imagined the life I have now. I look back and see all the small "coincidences" and experiences that shaped my path. Those books were meant to be taken out at the library, even though I wasn't exactly sure why I was borrowing them. I wasn't experiencing any paranormal activity and I wasn't seeing anything out of the ordinary. Perhaps it was my intuition guiding me to read those books. Maybe Divine guidance. Whatever the reason, as I look back, I realize these small steps of spiritual action were paving the way for something much bigger than myself.

My first experience with intuition happened the night before I had an appointment. I had the clearest dream of the inside of the office I would be visiting the next day. I saw the grass that was longer out front, the foyer of his home, the tall bookshelves that lined the walls, but the most impressive thing I clearly dreamed of were the tiny dragon figurines displayed around his home. All this and I had never stepped foot in his home. Imagine my surprise when I arrived at his home office and all the things I had predicted in my dream were real. Right down to the dragons!

This was my first clear step in realizing my underlying psychic gifts. I wasn't born to-do this. This is something I chose or rather, something that chose me. My intuition grew from that dream, although slowly. I didn't use it to my full capability nor did I realize that this was a super power. Me. Mom of three (soon to be four) kids. I had a super power within me that I didn't really know about let alone understand how to use I

We all have intuition built-in. It's the gut feeling or the knowing you have when you turn the wrong direction on a street or when you meet someone for the first time and something about them feels "off". That is the basic use of intuition. Tapping into that knowing fully opens the door for SO many unimaginable gifts and opportunities. Whether you're a stay at home mother or an engineer, we all possess the power to sense something. Some of us choose to leave it dormant and only use it for survival. Sadly, this is a waste of such a gift we are all born with.

Using this gift, stretching it, practicing with it, opening it, becoming aware, and trusting our intuition are all means of transforming our small gut knowing into something bigger. Perhaps becoming a Medium is something you would like to pursue. It is possible. You are all Mediums, because you are curious about the spirit world and how to connect with it. You intuitively know there is more than what you see with your eyes when you see a shadow out of the corner of your eye and nothing is there. When you hear a high-pitched ringing in your ear. When you feel a crawling of bugs sensation in your hair. You know it can be explained. Not by science but knowing. Feeling.

Believing is a by-product of consistent other- worldly experiences. The more you experience, the more you will believe. Can you jump in and believe you are a Medium? Or can you start by simply believing in your intuition? Let's start with baby steps and work our way up the spiritual ladder, shall we? I know you have it in you. It's only a matter of trusting in the unknown, the unseen, and the experiences that will shape this journey.

Every single human being has a soul and that soul has chosen to come here and do the work. You carry with you many lessons from past lives and have agreed to continue learning them throughout this lifetime. You have important work to do. It wasn't a coincidence that you found my book. It wasn't a coincidence that a friend suggested you go get it and read it. When you purchased it, you basically told the Universe, "I AM READY FOR SOMETHING NEW AND BIG."

The Universe is constantly trying to direct you in the best way that is always in the highest and best purpose for you. I want you to be proud of the fact that you listened to that guidance. Your intuition is growing and expanding as we speak. When you listened to that gut-feeling and said yes, you said yes to more than this book.

Although it IS an awesome book. You should buy more. Buy two and give it to your friend for their birthday. The first person who came to your mind is the one you give it to. Why? Because THAT is how this intuition stuff works. It's the knowing and that flash of a feeling, an image, or a nudge. Follow that. I know I am. Are YOU?

Are You Ignoring It?

If you are, that's ok. There is nothing wrong with that (unless you decide to date that rude person anyway because he's hot-oh wait, that's me.) The nudges are there for a reason. The basic purpose of your intuition is to keep you safe. We all ignore it sometimes. Buying the home that has unseen mold in the walls. Or that purchase you're about to make that has a hole in it and you aren't aware until you get home. These two things happened to me when I ignored my intuition.

The house was cute when we viewed it at *night time. In the dark.* And said yes while putting down first and last month's rent. Even though my mind screamed, DON'T! I totally ignored it because I was so focused on moving from our over- populated city to this quieter community. Not to mention I had a baby on the way. You get it. You've been there. It just wasn't ideal when on moving day, when in the light we found a whole whack of issues that we missed.

If I had listened to my gut, we may have waited a few more days and found a hole-free, mold-free home with fewer broken screen doors. Too late. You will thank yourself for deciding to go with your gut and taking this book home. You used your superpowers in the first small way.

Basically, You're Amazeballs

Yes, that's right, I said amazeballs. I totally went there. I'll probably do it again later. But really, I want to stress how amazing you truly are. I'm good at seeing the light in other people, especially the ones who don't think they are incredible. I see yours. But, if you hide your powers, the light within can't shine like it's meant to. If you don't talk about intuition, spirit, signs, messages, your loved ones in spirit, you're hiding. You may worry about what other people will think of you when you open your mouth and start spewing out ideas like, "Did you know we can co-create our life with source?" and "I have superpowers where I can magically manifest anything into my life."

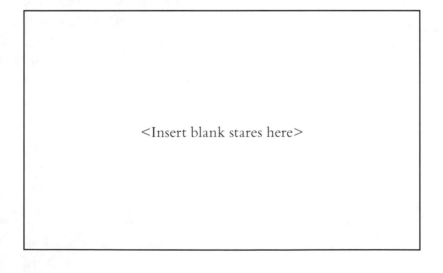

<Insert blank stares here>

You have incredible superpowers and they are meant to be shared. Period. You cannot hide the fact that there is more to this world than that nine to five job with that big corporation or that only physical things we see with our eyes are it. I'm telling you there is more. More abundance, more prosperity, more symbols, and more signs than you ever imagined. And it's all *within you.* You have the power to create anything with your thoughts, feelings, and actions. If that isn't true power, then I don't know what is.

This book is going to teach you how to do this. It's going to have you stretching, expanding, developing, and some more "ings" that I just forgot now. You will see the light that lives in you and then USE it out in the world. Notice I didn't say "real" world; that's a story and a whole other book I'm saving for later.

Maybe you don't see how this is truly possible just yet. We will get there. Because we all have this gift and we have had it since our diaper days. Do you remember how you knew your Mom was your Mom when you were born? Me either. But you had it. Do you remember how you knew you just had to buy that house, because it was SO you? That feeling is what we are going to work on. Each chapter will have your mind and your eyes blown so wide open you will never want to go back to "normal." Normal won't be an option anymore and you won't even care. We are going to unleash this power and once you decide to utilize it to its greatest capacity, you won't ever want to stop.

What's the next step? The first stage in our journey is going to become quiet. No, I don't mean a trip to the washroom without little kid hands wiggling under the door as you pee. It is an escape, just not that kind. As a last resort, you can do it in the washroom while you pee, which is weird but trust me it works. Oh, my Gawde the peace.

The next step is what will start the big changes in motion. It's a game changer, a life saver, and an all-time calmer-downer.

You cannot skip it. Don't go to chapter four. Seriously. This isn't a "Choose Your Own Adventure" book. Oh man, I did it again with another 90's reference.

I'll wait while you consult Google.

CHAPTER TWO

MEDITATION

"Meditation. Because some questions can't be answered by Google"

Meditation

I KNOW YOU *totally* want to skip over this chapter. No way. I'm not entirely sure what it is about this "M" word that has people running for the hills in terror. Is it the fear of being quiet for more than a minute and hearing their own thoughts or is it fear of the unknown? In my experience, my students are concerned with lack of time to do so and the worry that they will not be able to "turn off" their thoughts. Noted. All the above-mentioned excuses are valid. I hear ya, soul sister. It's not easy but let me tell you once you get past the fear, the excuses, and the worry, it will be one of the best life decisions you will have ever made.

My meditation routine began when I started my Mediumship classes. Day one of class, Teacher says to us all: "If you do not meditate, every single day, I will find out and know because you won't get better." I guessed I had better get busy. I haven't missed a day in over two years. Not because of fear of my teacher finding out that I wasn't, but because I really wanted to be a Medium. Badly. I decided to buckle down, commit and dive in. And you need all three of these driving forces if you want to do something huge like mediumship or psychic readings. Meditation is the ONLY way to get there. What if you just want to have a meditation routine for peace and calmness? Well, why don't we examine the benefits of meditation and you can decide for you self if it's for you or not.

PS. It is for you. Trust me. Your reasoning behind the decision to start doesn't matter. Just start.

I want to stress that meditation is not just for clearing a path to incredible things. Meditation is amazing for day to day "I'm having a stressful day," "get me out of here, I need to breathe" moments too. Having somewhere to just be quiet and consciously breathe in and out is a huge feat in and of itself. Think about your busy day. Are you really breathing or just surviving?

When you consciously make the effort to breathe in and out PROPERLY, you immediately feel the effects and can bring yourself back to the present. This is what we call mindfulness. Being present. Breathing in and out slowly. Remembering we are alive and feeling back into our bodies. Being mindful is one of the best ways to combat stressful situations. You can put your hand on your chest, feel your heart beating and just take a big breath in and let it out slowly. Go on! Try it right now. You may feel silly at first, but I tell you, it's huge. Bring yourself back to NOW. Because really, now is all we have. The past is gone. The future hasn't been determined yet, (well, depending what you believe to be truth ☺) so whatcha got left? NOW. Taking five minutes to close your eyes and shut that "reality" out can really get you far.

Imagine you are at work. Your co-workers are annoying you, your boss wants it yesterday, and it's still an hour away from lunch. All you want to do is pull your hair out and scream, you can't, but there IS something you CAN do. Excuse yourself to the washroom. Yes, we all should pee at some point. Go in the stall and lock the door. Take a deep breath in and hold it for 5 seconds. Then slowly like a balloon, let it out for the count of 8. Yes, I'm just randomly choosing numbers, but the numbers don't matter here. It's the act of taking a time out and doing something for you. Bringing yourself back to your body and being mindful and finding peace. Who wants peace? Show of hands. ME!

If meditating in the stall at work grosses you out and perhaps you are a germaphobe, go in your car. The reason I have all these awesome ideas is because I've done them. Yep. My teaching job was a) super stressful (you try controlling 30 five-year- old's) and b) I no longer wanted to be there. Like ever. I hated my job. So, what's a girl to do?

Lunch time was my favourite time of the day for me. It was when I got to breathe again. Calm myself down and be present. The rest of the time was me counting down the hours till I could go home (future) and wishing I was still in bed (past). and the only way to get through it was to breathe my car. Ahhh... Heaven. I began to look forward to not only lunch time but stealing a few moments alone in the car. No one saw me or watched me close my eyes and breathe so I sure didn't have to worry about what anyone thought of me. It was at those times that I really got present.

I stopped counting the hours left in the work day and instantly felt better. It allowed for me to remind myself that I was ok, and everything was cool beans. Because it really was. As I sit here now on my front porch with my laptop soaking up rays of sunshine and I can smile back at those bathroom stall/car breaks. I may no longer need them to get through my day, but I do still need my meditation fix. It's just for a different reason now. And there are many ways to meditate, too! Not just five minutes taking a deep breath. But hey, if you're doing that, bravo. I'm proud of you for taking five for you. If you can make that a routine, the benefits are even more long lasting and beneficial for you.

So how do you even do this anyway? Don't worry, I'll walk you through. I will have you craving this not dreading it or making it a chore. And it won't be just "one more thing you have to do today" either.

The first step is to choose a time. Don't even say I don't have time. You do. You have lots of it. You are awake for eighteen hours of it. Surely you can carve out ten minutes in that vast stretch of time. I always suggest to my students that they choose either right when they wake up (yes, before you check Facebook) or just before they go to bed at night. These are the easiest times to begin a new meditation practice. Easy is key to beginning. You don't want to do this at 2 pm when the kids are coming home soon or you're in a busy meeting. Start small and easy. Sound good?

Now that you've chosen am or pm, the best way to start is to grab your phone (that thing that's attached to your hand most of the day ☺) and some earbuds. YouTube has many timed meditations and I suggest you start with five minutes. You can google 5-minute meditation. Or even better, I highly recommend Insight Timer! You can keep track of your progress and choose from literally thousands of meditations. You will even get a nerdy bar graph of how many days you have meditated. Kind of keeps you accountable. Press play. Close your eyes and take three deep breaths in and out. That's it. Tell me when you're done. (Long pause)

Oh, you're back! Congratulations! You just finished your first meditation. The first one is usually the hardest because most of the work is DECIDING to start. Once you have made the decision to, it is smooth sailing from here on out. You've got this!

Now what? Tomorrow, either morning or evening, you're going to do this again. You can either do 5-minutes OR you can amp it up and be a rebel who chooses a 10-minute meditation. Either way, just do it.

Let's talk about the WHY. Why should I keep going? Why should I start? Because some Medium author told me to? If that's your WHY, then the minute you stop reading this book you will not do it anymore. It's got to be for YOU. You need to want to be able to sense things aside from wrong directional patterns on a road trip. The reason needs to come from wanting something *more.* Something more than what you've been experiencing your entire life. What if you keep doing this and you notice magic all around you or that your thoughts can manifest incredible opportunities and dreams right to you? I'm serious and I am for real! Therefore, I am so passionate about teaching people how to unearth their intuition.

The starting gate to greatness is through the power of meditation. Those car breaks I talked about earlier helped me get to where I am today. Five minutes of mindfulness was enough to remind me to stay in the present moment and to realize the abundance that is all round all of us. Even you! And who doesn't want magic? I do! Ok then, what are you waiting for?

What is your WHY for doing this? Even after this book is finished and you've lent it to the next person who could use some magical unearthing of their intuitive powers. Why do you want to keep going? What is in it for you? LOTS! Read on to find out how many great side effects there actually are.

Benefits of Meditation

There are so many, so I'll only list my favorite ones.

1. Primarily, you will find peace. And who doesn't want peace? Peace of mind, peace in your heart, your home, and in all your reactions to triggers. Instead of reacting, you will begin to respond. Whoever said, peace begins with you and other similar things are onto something.

Something big. Having a meditation routine sets the stage for peace to be found once again. You always have peace within. The reason it seems otherwise sometimes is our reaction to an external trigger is off. Our natural state of being is peace. Ahhh…peace! Go find it. It's in there somewhere. It's the silence you have lost amidst all the chaos and constant noise. It's going back to you. It's a little like going home or returning to a long-lost friendship. The tingles, the lack of chatter, the knowing that you're YOU. All of it will be found when you get peaceful and quiet.

2. Time for yourself. This is important, especially as women and mothers who are hard-wired to put ourselves last. Meditation is a way to carve out that ever-elusive Me time. Imagine this: Thirty minutes or more where you don't have to tend to a boo-boo, clean the house, scrub the toilet, and other mundane and not fun jobs we take on. Unless you're good at delegating, like me, and give those jobs to your hubby or kids. When you commit to meditating every day, not only do you receive peace, but you get to do something for YOU.

   When was the last time you did something good for you for YOU? You've heard that you can't pour from an empty cup and all that stuff. It's so true. In my experience, putting me last and forgetting I am a live person had many negative effects not only on me, but on my family. You notice how you react when you're frazzled, right? The more you meditate and make time for it, the less you will react to the little or bigger triggers in your day. The kids spilling milk everywhere (was that on purpose?) won't go from molehill to mountain in 1.9 seconds after a while. You will be able to calm and not react, but instead *respond* to it in an appropriate way now. That's one good why, if you ask me! Your kids will thank you for not freaking out on them, too.

3. Manage anxiety. Millions of people suffer from anxiety. It's a debilitating mental health issue that has people gasping for breath with crazy beating hearts and chest crushing pressure. It leaves them reeling from panic and social triggers. I have personally experienced these symptoms plus more, so I know firsthand how you feel. I've tried prescription drugs (no, thank you) and counseling to curb my anxiety woes and I can honestly tell you that my bouts of attacks have lessened if not almost completely stopped once I focused on breathing and meditating. Meditation has been a life saver to me. It forces you to breathe in controlled manner and to shut out the outside world and face what most of us fear: not being in control of ourselves and of the unknown.

   When you are in meditation, you no longer worry. You no longer fear. You can't, because you are not of this world and you are your truest self and in the present fully. Anxiety can be kicked to the curb at that exact moment. So long anxiety.

4. You are connected to Source. When I say Source, I am referring to the Universal energy. The big guy. The Universe. Spirit. God. Angels. Guides. You get the gist. You can call it whatever you wish if you realize this power is bigger than anything we can even fathom but are all a part of. Source energy is where we connect with a higher power and universal intelligence. This is the realm where we feel energy and can communicate with beings who have passed from this physical world. Think of Source

as a purple light that travels down from the Universe into the top of our heads and fills us up with immense spiritual knowledge. Cool, eh? Have I freaked you out yet? Hopefully not, because if you decide to work with spirit and open that channel, you'd better prepare for the most amazing and unexplainable relationship you all have. It's been there the whole time, I swear. Now get ready for that magical stuff I've mentioned before.

5. You become YOU. This is another powerful benefit to meditation. When I say become YOU, what I mean is when you get quiet and make a lifelong habit out of it, you become the truest version of yourself. The part of you that doesn't have constant noise, self-doubt, frustration, sadness, or guilt. When you are quiet for hours, you cannot be anyone else but YOU. Think about it. When you are sitting, doing absolutely nothing and all those annoying thoughts we attach ourselves to finally dissipate, that is true presence. We are being. Just that. And after a while, you won't be able to stop meditating because you feel so you. It's like you're an onion and the layers begin to peel off. You think you're already you, but there are more layers to unravel. Underneath all of what you know, is more of the real you. The mask will fall off and you will find that you no longer can pretend in social or private situation.

6. Higher Vibration. The more you meditate, think positive thoughts, and are kind to all, the higher your vibration rises. What I mean by that is every living organism has a vibration. We are all energy beings and emit a frequency or vibration. Consciously raising yours through meditative practices lifts you to a higher vibration. You smile more, love more, fear less, experience less frustration because

> you exude empathy for all. Lower vibrational friends and situations will naturally fall away from you and your old life. The higher you rise, the more aware of the spirit world you become. You will notice increasingly that assistance and opportunities which are for your highest and best will appear as if out of nowhere.

Truly, the list is endless. Infinite.

Whether you use meditation for peace and quiet, mindfulness, or you want to amp it up to a powerful thing that it is and manifest some cool stuff, any reason is a great reason. Your soul will thank you. Your friends and family will be happy you do. Most importantly, you will be doing something for YOU. You will no longer be an empty cup you try to pour from. You will have so much more to give to others, meditating is like filling up the gas tank in your minivan. You can't go very far when it's on empty. Fill it up to the brim. The more you meditate, the fuller your tank will be. You deserve every benefit, plus more I haven't even mentioned here. You're incredible and you deserve this. I see you and I know you. Clap for your damn self then go meditate. Again, and again. Tomorrow, the day after, and in the weeks after this book is done. It only takes 30 days to form a life-long routine. Stick with it. Reward yourself for it and step into the powerful being that you are. If you're a mom, you're already a superhero and I commend that, but from this day on, you will discover more super powers you didn't even know you had in you.

"It's got to be for YOU.
You need to want to be able to sense things aside from wrong directional patterns on a road trip. The reason needs to come from wanting something more."
–Unearth Your Intuition

CHAPTER THREE

WHAT THE HECK IS SOURCE?

"I really believe in the philosophy that you create your own universe. I'm just trying to create a good one for myself."
-Jim Carrey

What Is Source?

BEFORE WE CAN jump into trusting, you need to know WHO or WHAT you are about to put your full trust into and on top of all that, it's invisible. It's not a person you can chat with, or sip tea with. How's that for an interesting relationship you're about to enter?

But first, I need to introduce you. It would be weird to set you two up and you don't know anything about one another! You can't lurk on it like a dating profile, scroll through its Facebook page or LinkedIn site to stalk–I mean look at. Since Source is invisible, you can't shake its hand or give it a hug. Think of it as the most fabulous first date you've ever been on. I'm going to describe Source as a person or first date prospect because 1) It's easier and 2) I like the humour.

Listen up. I have this friend that would be *perfect* for you. I've only known this friend since I was born, but I didn't really notice them until I was 38! Can you believe that? How did I not realize they existed and how freaking amazing they are until I was 38? Well, that is when I had what we like to call, my spiritual awakening. Sounds dramatic, doesn't it?

When you realize who Source really is, you usually go through a huge loss or devastating event. Mine was both. Source totally showed up right when I needed them. The funny part is, they said, "Dude, we've been here the entire time. You just didn't know it."

Source is the highest and purest form of all- time ultimate energy, abundance, and life-force. You can call it Source, God, Divine, Allah, the Universe, whatever you feel most comfortable with. You need to believe in something, right? This can't be all us.

Source is the most powerful magical force that has literally been swirling round the Universe and thus us for billions of years. I feel like Source is the hottest, smartest, toughest, most generous, magical guy at school and we should all be swooning over him. If I tell you he's rich and can make you rich too, does that help? I swear I'm not lying. How can we not all be dating this one? Hell, I want to marry him.

Source is the ultimate universal energy that we all have in our lives. All we must do is say yes and reach out our hand to it. Grab on tight. It's going to be the best first date you ever had. Period.

Reader, I'd like you to meet Source.

Source, Reader.

Here we go…

Spirit in The Sky

Now that I've introduced you to Source, the ultimate marrying partner, let's move onto Spirit. I like to use the term Spirit when talking about a loved one in Spirit, a Spirit Guide, a Spirit animal. You get the drift. Spirit goes hand in hand with Source because of its light energy and ultimate invisible powers. Spirit can't be seen, but it sure can be heard, and felt.

Have you ever felt the hair on your arms stand up suddenly? That's Spirit. Most likely a loved one who has passed over and is now on the other side. Or perhaps you've felt an energetic presence near or beside you. That is Spirit as well. Now Spirit isn't limited to just a loved one who is no longer physically present.

Let's talk about my favourite topic first. You all know what a Medium does. As a Medium, some of my favourite peeps are the ones who have passed over. Obviously, I'm all about the invisible and everything that you cannot see with your eyes. The stuff that is pure energy, yet still delivers a powerful message through me to you. Spirit communicates and conveys to me through validation. They tell me all about themselves, how they passed over, important dates, and my personal fave, what they've seen you do lately.

Oh, and Spirit can be hilarious as me! And they *are* funny too. More on what Spirit does in the last few chapters. I'm saving the good stuff for last. Hey. No skipping over to the last chapter. It's super important to read these in order. Unless you're a rule breaker, then ok fine, go ahead. Just don't ruin it for the other readers.

Spirit Guides

Spirit Guides are beings who are with us our entire lives and have been specifically assigned to us. Their job is to, well, um, guide us and give us, guidance along the way in this lifetime.

Spirit Guides work alongside our intuition. The gut-feeling and Guides team up and *try* to show us what is best and where we should be heading. Sometimes literally.

Once I was driving to a client's home for a reading and their street extended both north and south in my town. Even the numbers on the houses were the same both ways. As I was driving, and decided to turn right, I heard this very loud voice in my head (that's where you might hear the guidance) "YOU'RE GOING THE WRONG WAY!" as if a regular human was sitting in the passenger seat beside me and yelling in my right ear. Aaaaand of course, like most of us do, I ignored them. Total blatant disregard. I turned right anyway, rebel that I am. And look where it got me. You can probably guess. The wrong house. With the wrong person. I even ignored my Guides while walking up the wrong driveway and when the wrong man opened the wrong door.

What I probably should have done is listened to the GUIDANCE. As I type this, my Guides are shaking their heads at me saying, "We told you so!" Awesome. Got it. Won't happen again.

Right. It'll totally happen again. We think we know better. We're the human in this relationship who is ego-minded and love to be in control. Why would we let some invisible beings who are supposedly "helping us" run this show? If you use my example of why, then you have your answer. Get to know your Spirit Guides. They can be your BFF and only want what is best for you. They'll show you the way if you allow it. Just because you can't see something doesn't mean it doesn't exist. Who yelled in my ear that day in the car? Spirit Guides! They know stuff and once you understand they are here to guide you, you may want to listen to them or you'll end up going the wrong way. Literally.

Spirit Animals/Totems

I love Spirit Animals. They're cute and fuzzy. I want to squeeze them and love them. Oh wait. That's *puppies*. I want to squeeze puppies. You can't cuddle a Spirit Animal. That would be weird because sometimes they are invisible too, but not always. Let me explain.

Just like with Spirit Guides, you've been assigned specific Spirit Animals. I guess Source decided we needed a whole team on our side, cheering us on and giving us guidance our whole time on this planet. Nailed it. Some smart beings to guide us and some important animals that represent us.

Let's start with the animal that is on our team. For me, that animal is a Crow. A crow represents magic and is a majestic and super smart animal. I was given a crow to remind me that there is magic all around. Not only around me, but in me. I am a super powerful manifesting agent and can magically manifest abundance into my life, ***simply by thinking or speaking it***. Bam.

Magic is a perfect theme for me as well. Having the ability to converse with the other side successfully is incredibly magical, not to mention an important gift that I am meant to share.

These animals act and serve as important reminders and encompass the best parts of us. Do you know what yours is? I am grateful to know mine. You can find out what yours is through a specific guided meditation.

The other side (pun intended) of that is sometimes you will be given a different spirit animal which is usually referred to as a totem which brings specific messages to you as needed. Say for instance you are seeing a whole whack load of dragonflies all around you. Well, lucky for you, dragonflies represent transformation!

Source will deliver these to you when they are trying to let you know you're about to be transformed by an event or upcoming decision you may need to make. And like always, use your intuition primarily when noticing these spirit animals.

They too, bring magic and messages. There is no coincidence to these animals crossing your path. Sometimes it's helpful to have a book to refer the animal meaning and message behind it.

There is an excellent book you can check out: Spirit Animals by Dr. Steven Farmer. You can also Google, but unfortunately not all sites have the same meanings and that can be confusing. Go with your gut. Always. These amazing creatures are always around us, giving us guidance and meaning that will always be true for you at the time.

Thinking of making a change? Butterflies will show up. Cardinals will show up as your loved one in Spirit wants to say hello. Trusting these animals takes time, but after a while and as your meditation practice grows and develops, you will notice them more and they may show up in your alone time.

You Talk to Invisible People?

YES! This is one of my favourite parts of the book because I am in love with all that I cannot see. No, I am not crazy, (*although some logical, science- brained folks may seriously* consider *having me put in a straight jacket*). I don't mind. I love what I do and that is all that matters. You don't have to believe me, and I don't have to prove it to you. My job is to provide the messages from them and then YOU decide if you believe or not. I never want to force my beliefs on you just like I'd never want you to do that to me. All I can do is provide the best service and share the important messages with you. The rest is up to you.

All of what I have discussed in this chapter really seems to focus on invisibility. If something is invisible, does it mean it's not there?

Think about air you breathe. Can you see it? Ok, only when it's freezing outside, but you know it's there and its invisible. You have proof it's there because its science and stuff. My invisible is harder to prove because of the non-science explanation.

Consider energy. You know it's all around you. You can feel it in your body, the energy when you rub your hands together and pull them part. That's Reiki. And Reiki isn't science but a powerful modality that millions have used to assist them in their healing processes. My point is, it's all invisible, whether it's a scientifically proven fact or metaphysical. Both are legit. Not too legit. They won't quit or anything. You may want to quit this book because of my bad jokes but keep reading. We're about to blow your mind in the next chapter.

If you aren't open to all I've discussed up until now, this relationship just can't work. It won't work. You'll have to break up with this new relationship before it even gets to the good part. If you'll take a big leap of faith and give the invisible a go, we can go far in our journey.

There is power in invisible. The most incredible parts of our lives come from magic, which cannot be seen. There is so much more to this life than what you think you know to be true. If you dig down a little deeper, you may feel or sense this notion under the surface. That's how I got to this point in my life.

One day I had THE MOMENT. That moment I realized there must be more to life than this as my toddler is in full-blown temper tantrum mode and is wreaking havoc on my living room with his two thousand Legos. Remember, you put on the cape in chapter one. Don't chicken out now and stuff it back under your clothes. You'll want to see how this plays out.

The Most Powerful Relationship You'll Ever Have

I'm so glad I set you and Source up. How's the first date going? Did he flash a big wad of cash at you? (Abundance) Did he direct you on which way was the best way to travel to your destination? (Intuition) Isn't he handsome? He has a super powerful, magnetic personality and everyone wants to be around him. I forgot to mention one thing. You're going to have to share him. It's for the highest good and what's best of all of you, the collective consciousness. We are all in this together. We are all one, and all that jazz.

What you're doing together is big. You and others are co-creating together. You're all in. Now that you and Source are getting to know each other better, you will need to know that you are a powerful, magical team. You are getting all the rewards here. Not only are you going to have a second date, but I think I'll hear wedding bells soon. You're going to want to move super-fast here, because the sooner you realize the magnetism of your togetherness, the more you'll create a completely different life for yourself.

Source will show you that you are not limited like you've believed. He will bring out the best in you and allow you to be your complete truest self. No one will be superior to you anymore as you step into your powers with love, not fear. In fact, in this relationship, fear will magically melt away, so you can make more love-based decisions which will bring you the most joy. That is the goal of this relationship. Of any relationship, but this one takes the wedding cake. I mean cake.

Think of all the possibilities available to you now. Truthfully, they always were available to you, but you hadn't realized, or maybe you did, you just didn't tap into it fully. By entering this relationship, you have stepped into your magic.

You've always had the magic in you. I think that's a song lyric. Or a Harry Potter quote. Oh, Harry Potter. Another of my favourites next to invisible people. Am I allowed to mention Harry Potter in my book? Let's try it out. Muggle. Ron. Hermione. Dumbledore. <waits>

I guess I can! The reason I do is because that book and movie represents how you probably feel or felt before you bought this book. A Muggle.

No one, not even you, understood the magic within. You felt it lurking without being sure what it was or how to deal. Lucky for you, no one is going to stuff you in a cupboard under the stairs to hide this magic (intuition).

You now have a magic wand in your hand.

I'm not kidding. It may be invisible too but it's there. Every word you speak and every thought you have is like a powerful magic spell. More on that in Chapter Five: The Law of Attraction. You've started a strong force in motion here on this first date and everything is about to change.

Say good bye to your Muggle-ness.

In the next chapter, we will learn to begin to trust Spirit. We will ask for a sign and start to find our faith in our new-found relationship together.

"Get to know your Spirit Guides. They can be your BFF and only want what is best for you. They'll show you the way if you allow it. Just because you can't see something doesn't mean it doesn't exist."

CHAPTER FOUR

TRUST

"Trust me, I know what I am doing."-Universe

Signs from a Friend

NOW THAT WE'VE establish what Source is and what it's all about, the next step is to put our faith pants on and begin to build some trust. You trusted yourself to meet up, trusted me to introduce something to you that knew would be in your best interest, and trusted in me, as an author of this book, to give you what you were looking for. Source and I haven't given you reason to trust us yet. We may be some Joe or Jane Blow off the street. Why should you trust us? That is where faith comes in handy.

It's helpful to note that trust is a two-way street. As you know from a regular relationship, it's all about give and take. You need to show up, be truthful in your words and actions, and share just like you would with your spouse. Now that you and Source are already on your way to being hitched, this makes total sense.

Let me share an example of building trust with Source in the early days of our courtship.

Being a newbie to this awareness of the Universe and its almighty power, I wanted to test out the waters. Put it to the test. Give it a whirl. Take it for a test drive. Ok I'll stop.

How did I know what I was experiencing was real? How did I know it wasn't my imagination or just a coincidence? SO, I asked for a sign. Not just any sign. A sign on what to do next. What did I need to learn about my new friend that would help me understand better? I put the intention out there, asked for a sign and BAM I got it. Literally in my lap. My sign appeared to me in book form. Yawn. Sounds boring, but it's not.

I was at a good friend's house for a tea date and I asked if she had any good books for me to read. (Because you know, a Mom of four kids has time to read. No really, I do. Now. Not when they were little, but I love to read!)

She said, "Oh! I have some books I'm getting rid of because I'm moving. You can have them if you want. Now being a bookworm, I *never* say no to books. She plucked this one book off the shelf and put it in my lap. I looked down at the cover and the title read: *The Everything Law of Attraction Book*. Huh. Now I realize this isn't the Law of Attraction chapter, (that's next), but it totally fits here because 1) I intended and asked for a sign and 2) I was beginning to trust in Source to hand- deliver to me. This was a HUGE sign, although I didn't realize it at the time. I took the book home and began to read it immediately. An exercise in trust. I could have put the book on the shelf or in a box to donate. But something in me (Intuition) told me this was important. It was only the first of the many signs I'd receive from Source from that day on.

it? It was too phenomenally orchestrated to be coincidence. Side note: there is no such thing as coincidence so put that away in your back pocket if that is what you've heard your entire life.

Do you get it yet? Not only did I ask for that to occur, but it physically manifested into my life. It was for my highest good and the Universe loved me so much that it practically put my request on speed- dial and priority post shipped it to me in three hours. Three hours! Here I sit reveling in this huge exercise in trust and grateful that the Universe thought so highly of me that it over-delivered the sign.

Signs From a Friend

It's also helpful to note that trust is a two-way street here. You can't have it be just one-sided. It doesn't work that way. As you know of course from a regular human relationship you've had and currently have now. It's all about give and take, showing up, being truthful in your words and actions, sharing just like you would with your spouse. And now that you and source are already on your way to being hitched, this makes total sense. Maybe.

Let me share an example of building up trust with Source in the early days of our courtship.

Being newbie to this brand-new awareness of the Universe and its almighty power, I wanted to test out the waters so to speak. Put it to the test. Give it a whirl. Take it for a test drive. Ok ill stop. How did I know what I was experiencing was real? How did I know it wasn't my imagination and that it wasn't just coincidence in what was about to occur? SO, I asked. For a sign. Not just any sign. A sign on what to do next. What did I need to learn about my new friend that would help me understand better? I put the intention out there, asked for a sign and BAM. I got it. In my lap. Literally. My sign appeared to be in book form. Yawn. Sounds boring? It's not.

I was at a good friend's house for a tea date and I started asking if she had any good books for me to read. (Because you know, a Mom of four kids has time to read. No really, I do. Now. Not when hey were little but I love to read!) She said, "Oh! I have some books I m getting rid of because I'm moving. You can have them if you want. Now being a bookworm, I *never* say no to books. She plucked this one book off the shelf and put it in my lap. I looked down at the cover and the title read: *The Everything Law of Attraction Book.* Huh. Now I realize this isn't the LOA chapter, (that's next) but it totally fits here because 1) I intended and asked for a sign and 2) I was beginning to trust in Spirit/ Source to hand- deliver to me.

This was a HUGE sign although I didn't' realize it at the time. I took it home and began to read it immediately. An exercise in trust. I could have put the book on the shelf or in a box and donated it. But something in me (intuition) told me this was important. It was only the beginning of the many signs I would be receiving from spirit/source from that day on.

Testing the Water

I know I sound like a broken record but if you don't trust, you can't manifest or receive signs fully. Heck, you probably won't even notice many of them. And they are ALL AROUND YOU. Everywhere. It's like that song by Tesla, "Signs, signs everywhere the signs!" PS I love that song. Abundantly given, more than enough for everyone who asks. Because source is infinite. It's in everything and everyone. Even you. And the sooner you realize this incredible information as truth, the easier it will be to receive the signs and accept them fully as real. Great, now I have that song stuck in my head. Quick! Sing something else!

If you're feeling a little cheeky and saucy, we can do a little test just to see if what I'm feeding you isn't total bullshit. Its not but you can see for yourself. So, we can test the universal waters and ask for a sign. Do you want to know a secret? Spirit and source have a sense of humour. Yep. You'll see. For me, I asked for a sign that what I was doing was on the right track. As I was driving home a little while after asking, a truck drove past me and I swear on my kids, it said "If you're looking for a sign, this is it." No joke. Ha-ha very funny. Ok I got my sign. And I had to trust in that. I may not have received it in the way I expected, but I got it. With a twist. And that is how the Universe works.

When you ask for a sign, the key is to expect the unexpected. You gotta let go of control of HOW it's going to come and in what form. Because I'm telling you, signs come in many ways. You can't control when. You can't control where. You can't control how its going to show up. Part of trust is asking and then waiting to see what the other person does with it. And the most important thing I need to stress is that THE UNIVERSE WILL NEVER LET YOU DOWN. It only wants what is best for you. The highest and best. So, trust that shit. Trust the sign that says, I'm a sign, here it is. You asked for it. You got it. Delivered.

Another part of trust to appreciate and give gratitude for the sign once you have received it. If someone give you a gift, do you throw it on the floor right in front of them? Or do you say, "Wow thanks! You gave me what I asked for! Thank you! I trust you'll deliver when I ask for help!" This is SO important. Not that the universe will give up on you, but appreciation goes along way in any relationship. You'll get more out of it. What you put into something, is what you get out of it. So, give it a big thank you! You're the best! More please! And watch the signs roll in like clockwork. Expect it but trust it too. You're welcome.

Ask and You Will Receive

This summer, like most summers, traveling to Niagara Falls, Ontario has become a family road trip tradition. It started when my oldest was young and his birthday falls in July. A birthday excursion has led to many more and this summer was no exception. The day we left, I was wondering why I hadn't heard back from my publisher after leaving a message a week or so before. I knew I wanted to go ahead with this, but on the inside, I was freaking out and afraid of saying a full-blown yes. For starters, the money was weighing on me. it wasn't five dollars to sign up, which would have been so easy! The second part was I was trusting in source that if this was for my highest and best on my path and a book was to be a part of it, things would happen. Trust, Jen, trust. As we loaded up the SUV, I said in my head, "OK give me a sign in eights that I am mean to write this book." Eights being instant manifestation and a big fat YES from the universe. Then, I let it go, which is a BIG part of the process. (More on that in the next chapter.)

I decided wasn't going to chase them or call again bugging them to have me. About halfway to our destination, I receive a message from someone who was already involved in the program I wanted to join.

> His message read:
> Him: "Have you heard from Nancy yet?"
> Me: 'Nope. I've got big chunk of moola just sitting in my bank account still."
> Him: "OK one sec. I'm going to call her now."
> Me: <Holy crap, is this really happening>
> Him: <Five minutes later> "She's going to call you right now."
> Me: "WHAT?"

And then, just like that, the phone rings.

OH, the magic of the universe and all it's workings isn't over yet.

Universe: "You want a sign in 8's? Well, Ima gonna give you some 8's!"

As we got out of the car and started walking out of the parking lot, we came up to a place that rents out motorized scooters. Can you guess where I'm going with this? Every single one of those scooters had a phone number on them and the first three numbers were "888." There must have been 100 scooters sitting there right in front of me. I regret not taking a photo to show you this incredible sign. I mean, 100 actual little signs right there.

All of this occurred within a span of maybe two-three hours after I asked the Universe to give me a sign that I was meant to write this book and take this amazing program. Between the asking, the phone call, and one hundred 888's, it was easy for me to trust. How could I ignore it? It was too phenomenally orchestrated to be coincidence. Side note: there is no such thing as coincidence so put that away in your back pocket if that is what you've heard your entire life. Do you get it yet? Not only did I ask for that to occur, but it physically manifested itself into my life. It was for my highest good and the Universe loved me so much put my request on speed-dial and priority post shipped it to me in 3 hours. 3 hours! Here I sit reveling in huge exercise in trust and am so grateful that the universe thought so highly of me that it over-delivered.

Feeling the Love

When it's your birthday (If it really is your birthday, man those psychic powers come in handy!) you obviously receive gifts. Gifts are the best part about birthdays! PS For my birthday please send money. If there is something you really want for your birthday, you probably do one of two things: Drop a lot of hints to your significant other or unassuming family member OR you just flat out ask for what you want. (More on specificity for your requests to the Universe in the next chapter) If you're like me, I usually start out with the first one. But then I see I may end up with an ugly gift I don't want and decide for the more logical approach. Direct. This is what I want. Here is the link, it's only

59.99 and it would go perfect in my wardrobe. Done. I know I will get that exact thing for my birthday because a) my hubby is the best and always gets me what I ask for on my birthday and b) I want to make sure I'm not disappointed with something close to it.

If you were taught well as a child and raised with deeply instilled manners like I was, (thanks mom!) you know that when it's your birthday and everyone is showering you with affection and gifts (plural), you don't just throw a temper tantrum when one of the gifts wasn't exactly what you asked for or how it got to your house that day. Imagine opening your gift and instantly frowning. Throwing the package on the ground stomping your feet yelling, "THIS IS TOTAL BULLSHIT! I DIDN'T ASK FOR THIS SWEATER. IT WASN'T WRAPPED PROPERLY, AND I WON'T WEAR IT. IT CAME FROM THAT STORE I HATE AND IF YOU THINK I AM SAYING THANK YOU FOR IT YOU'RE NUTS!" Whoa ok. Psst! This is what so NOT what to do when you get a gift from your hubby or the Universe. You were raised better than that, I hope. If this is you, I'm calling your Mother.

All kidding aside, normal people usually say thank you. Thank you for the sweater/gift goes a long way. Your giver feels good about this sweater for you that they lovingly and painstakingly scoured for hours in that busy mall you love. Imagine if she handed it over and you did the above. Same goes for the universal gifts that you request. Giving gratitude is SO important. It tells the Universe that you would like it to keep being awesome and give you more amazing special deliveries and not just on your birthday. Imagine gifts being showered upon you daily. Daily. That's every single day! And you can have these gifts on speed dial ***If*** you just tap into your superpowers. It's up to you if you let go of how and say a big thank you to the universe when the presents start pouring in. Thank you, Universe for bringing me the path to writing this amazing and helpful book for these readers!! More, please!

Superpowers Unfold Before Your Eyes

Ready to launch your very own superpowers? Get out that cape, my dear reader. I've got your first assignment.

Here is what I want you to do:

1. Ask the Universe for a feather/dime. Either out loud or in your head. Intention is key
2. Wait.
3. Trust
4. Receive.

Phew that was tough. I'm tired from all that super powering. OK well, that chapter's over. Just kidding. Then, when you get it, I want you to take a photo of it and show all your friends. Tell them what how freaking magical you are. Tell 'em the Universe and you are joined at the hip. Because you are. You aren't lying. You guys are one now and you're getting married. I'm so glad I set you two up! I'm the best match-maker ever.

You have this incredible ability to ask, believe, receive. We are all like that. Every single one of you, even that guy who didn't buy my book. It's ok I'll forgive him. Just this once. If you always think of this as putting in an online order or if you're old-school like myself and enjoy top forty hits from the 80's and 90's and prefer Sears catalogue, you'll get your order every time. The only time you may not receive it is if you DOUBT. That fear-based emotion where you have difficulty believing in the invisible. You are science-y and logic-minded and can't wrap your head around asking the big ole Uni to give you a gift. BTW, you are also asking your loved ones in Spirit for this gift. They hear you, too and want only what makes you smile. So, if a feather is what you wish for, a feather is what they will send.

I love this stuff so much and I love reading the reactions of my students and clients when we do this challenge. Some can't believe it and others are SO over the moon that Spirit heard them. How is this possible? Hey, I'm not Jen Nye the Science Guy and they don't tell me how it works. Why should I care? I trust this So much that I'm urging you to try it for yourself. Remember I said, my job is to show you the way, not force my beliefs on you. All you have to do is think it. You don't even have to write anything down like those other books make you do and you skip over with a guilty conscious thinking I'll do it later. I won't make you do that and it's not necessary for this exercise. You can do it as you read this book, you can do it lying down, you can do it at work. There is no excuse here. It's only a thought. Send it out. Give those superpowers a whirl. You will be amazed at your power and the results. In the next chapter, we are going to dive into even MORE signs that are available to you when you really open your eyes and take notice!

CHAPTER FIVE

SIGNS AND REPEATING NUMBERS

"Signs and symbols rule the world, not words nor laws."
- Confucius

You Need to Try This

IN MY COURSE, *Unearth Your Intuition*, one of the many ways I teach the importance of ***trusting*** in the invisible is through a powerful challenge. I like to call it *#featherchallenge*. The way I've set it up is to show my students that everything you ask for, whether in thought form or by speaking aloud, is heard from the Universe. Think of the universe as the ultimate Sears Wish Catalogue. If you're under the age of 25, I suggest we think of this as Amazon.ca. It doesn't matter which one you use, they both work the same.

As you know, when you are going to order something from that thick book of Christmas wishes or online, you know exactly what you are going to order. In this scenario, the wish book or Amazon is now the Universe/Source. You follow? Good. Let's say I want to order, oh I don't know, a feather. Right, I know you can't order a feather from Amazon. Why not? They have everything else. OK fine. Let's order a sweater. A lovely, cozy feather. I mean, sweater. Fill out the form (Sears Wish Catalogue) or type in "sweater" (feather) in the search bar at the top of the Amazon page. Put it in your "cart" (Ask aloud, "Can I please have a feather?"). Ok I will wait while you pay (ask the Universe) <Elevator music plays>. PERFECT. Done? Now what happens next? You wait.

When order something, you put the order in, you KNOW it's coming, and you have no doubt it will arrive in a timely manner. Unless it gets lost in Newfoundland and they've lost the tracking number. Bad example. I bring that up because I'm still bitter about these cool Hippie sweaters I bought but never received. The point is, YOU WILL RECEIVE THE DARN SWEATER (feather). How do I know? Because you placed an order with the Universe. The ultimate Amazon.ca and Sears Catalogue. They work the same way in that you will be delivered what you order. My students and clients have all done this exact exercise in TRUST and all have received their cool feathers. Then I ask them to post the photos of their special deliveries and we celebrate their immense superpowers and thank spirit for bringing them.

Now, another question I get from some people is, "How do I know it's not just a bird leaving a random feather on my doorstep that was jammed in the door frame clearly for me to see when I walked out to my car?" Ummmm, hellooooooooooo! Yes, because a bird walked right up to your door and stuffed it in there

BY MISTAKE. I get it. You didn't see the feather get there. Why should you believe in the miracle that is Source?

Remember I said, there is no such thing as coincidence and you put in your order. You put in your order and you let it go. You didn't ask Sears or Amazon, "How do you get that sweater in the package? Which shipping company are you using? Who picks the sweater off the shelf?" The Universe doesn't like when you ask HOW. Don't ask how. It doesn't matter how. Just trust it like you would these companies (the Universe) to deliver and it will arrive. Guaranteed.

Signs that are available to you when you really open your eyes and take notice!

Signs from Spirit

It would probably make more sense if you knew what the most common signs Source and the Universe are likely to give to you. Don't only go by my list here. There are many more and I want you to trust if you think something is a sign, then it is. Sensing what is a sign is a great way to trust. Here are a few that pop up most often and seem to be the favourites, if you will. Let's talk about Universal signs and then I will talk about Spirit signs. And yes, there is a difference.

Obstacles

Remember how I said Source/the Universe is *always* looking out for your best interest? Well, this goes right along with giving you signs. Right now, I'm sure you can think of a few that have already been sent as obstacles along your path. You ask for a sign that tonight's blind date is the right choice. Then suddenly your phone stops working, you feel sick to your stomach, or you rip your pantyhose (do people even wear pantyhose anymore?). If you do make it to your car, the battery is dead, or you have a flat tire. Do you see a theme here? The Universe is telling you "Do not go on this date." TRUST these signs! This may not be the answer you were hoping for, but alas you're getting it. The Universe loves you SO much it will do anything to assist you.

Butterflies

Butterflies have dual meaning. I always suggest when you see one that you use your INTUITION to determine which message is being brought to you in that moment. They signify both a loved one in Spirit is saying hello and wants you to know they are always with you and change. Think of a butterfly and how it begins as a caterpillar and transforms into this beautiful flying creature that can soar and fly now! Have you been feeling like things have changed or transformed for you in some way? Is everything about to change in your life? I bet you're noticing an influx of butterflies!

What about when it's winter and there are no butterflies to be seen? I get this all the time! You can notice butterflies anywhere; they don't have to be the insect flying around you. Photos will pop up, words others speak in conversation, paintings, figurines, images on t-shirts as you shop...(Animal totems) You get the idea. Spirit will deliver. Don't worry about how. When you ask, you'll receive. Just trust.

On my Facebook page, Mom to Medium Jen Abra, I recently offered an opportunity for my followers to ask Spirit for a butterfly. I called it hashtag butterfly challenge. I was overwhelmed with the amount of participation and videos from people who asked their loved one in spirit for a butterfly to come near him and it worked!!!! Well, I knew it would, but I really wanted others who may doubt this truth to know for sure.

Feathers

A feather is one of the most common sign a loved one in spirit will leave you. Again, if you ask for one, you will receive it. (#feather challenge) I offered the same challenge on my page and never anticipated the response I would get, even weeks after it was over. Feathers are everywhere yes, I know. Do you have faith in the invisible or are you too caught up in your head?? Bird feathers of all kinds will show up when you're walking, at the beach, in your home as you clean or walk up the stairs, on the coffee table and even on your blanket when you wake up. What a cool way to wake up. I even once found a blue jay feather on the seat of my SUV after locking it with all the windows closed. There it was waiting for me in plain sight when I returned. Explain that one. If that doesn't make you trust, I don't know what will!

Dimes

Another favourite gift from above. Spirit has told me during readings that it is more difficult for them to leave a dime and that's why they want you to pick it up. This goes for the feathers as well. Think about it for a second. Spirit is invisible. A dime is a metal object. Their energy would have to deliver one, so you will hopefully notice they are here. A gift from heaven. So, when you get one, trust it was meant for you to find. If you find one, pick it up. And don't forget to say thank you!

Songs

This is probably one of my most favourite signs form Spirit. Dual meaning is probable. Let me explain: Spirit is a high-vibe frequency and your deceased loved ones vibrate at a much higher rate than we are capable of and that's why we cannot see them. As with all frequencies, it is energy. Think of a radio, which operates on a different frequency we cannot see, but we know it works because we hear the music. If you're old school like me, you remember the dial on old car radios. When you "tune-in" to your favourite station, it's clear and has your favourite songs. When you turn it just a bit, you hear static. Since Spirit is a higher frequency, it can deliver those special meaningful songs right to you.

There are two ways you receive messages from Spirit.

Firstly, Spirit tries to give you an important message to guide you on your next steps through repetitive themes in song lyrics. Best way to hear messages in songs is to hit scan and listen. Do you hear a repeating theme of specific words? Maybe the songs playing are trying to tell you something.

Here is an example: This past year, I gave up doing something I loved. Zumba and dancing have been my passion for many years. I would go to class on a regular basis and even became an instructor, but life changes had stopped me. Yikes, right? I quit my membership. Lately, I've ben hearing songs with the word "dance" in them. "I Wanna Dance with Somebody" by Whitney Houston. "Everybody Dance Now" by C and C Music Factory. You get the drift. I must hear these types of songs ten or more times a day. Spirit knows this is for my highest good and wants me to go back. Maybe one day I'll go back ☺

The second way is through a specific song from your loved one in Spirit. Usually a favourite song of your loved one or a song you sang together while they were still physically here. If your loved one had a super strong personality, you can bet you will hear that song, sometimes repeatedly. They know everything and use the power of song to let you know they are ok and with you.

When you see a medium, a lot of the time, your loved one in spirit will validate that song or mention it. Specific Christmas songs, oldies, or recent Top 40, it doesn't matter. If it's a song they know you relate to them, they will tell the Medium so you will have no doubt they are present. They don't want you to be sad. They want to see you smile and have joy. For you to celebrate them is what makes them happy. If a specific song is what it takes to do that, they will give it to you. So, tune in to your favorite radio station and wait. It will be there and when it plays, crank it up and sing along!

No Such Thing as Coincidence

There's just not. You've heard this saying before or perhaps you live at the other end of the spectrum and feel like every person you meet or "run into" can be logically explained. I'm going to assume if you've picked up this book and are still reading it, you're the first type. If you think logically, this entire book will not resonate with you at all. Some of you were taught to doubt everything. To seek out proof. And my personal favorite: I'll believe it when I see it. Ugh.

This entire time, I've spoken to the people who *want* to believe in the invisible. Those who have faith or even the slightest bit of hope there is more to this world then what we can see or have known our entire lives. This book is for the ones who will see it WHEN they believe it. It takes a lot of faith and trust to go this route. To literally go forward blindly with little proof that the invisible, the Universe, Source, or Spirit even exist. The entire concept of my book focuses on trust. If you don't have trust, how can you believe coincidence isn't real?

Again, I never want to force my truth or belief on you. My trust may differ from yours. We have different belief systems because we were brought up differently. Now that you're an adult, you can make your own decisions and even change your beliefs if you so choose. Only you can decide what is true for you. I am going to keep assuming you believe in the information in this book or you would have thrown it out by now. Hopefully you haven't. If you did, you can't read this sentence anyway. I'm speaking to the ones who really wanted to read it.

Thanks, by the way. I love that you trusted me enough to share all the spiritual truths with you. This book is really a big summary of what I've learned over the past few years Yet even before my transition, I always knew there was no such thing as coincidence. Fate, serendipity, call it what you want. The wording doesn't matter.

This morning I posted yet another challenge for manifesting a dragonfly. Dragonflies symbolize transformation. As I mentioned in my live video, your words and thoughts instantly manifest. When I say instantly, I mean literally ten minutes later. I asked Spirit for a dragonfly, went outside to eat my breakfast on the front porch, and bam. A dragonfly. I didn't have my phone so I rushed inside to grab it, praying the dragonfly would still be there. When I went back out, it hadn't moved. Phew! Coincidence, I think not.

Was it coincidence that I asked for a dragonfly and it appeared so quickly? If you trust and believe in Spirit with your entire heart and soul, you will know it was called to you and you manifested it. The more you believe something will appear, the quicker it comes to you. The Universe doesn't work in coincidences. It doesn't even know what that means. It's a universal orchestration from the divine workings of Source and all of its powerfulness and abundance. Try it for yourself, if you're still not convinced. That helpful person who "appeared" out of "nowhere", the surprise money you received in your bank account, the empty lineup lane at the drive-through. All part of what you believed and manifested with your thoughts. The Universe delivered. All in the right time.

Number signs

I know you've seen repeating number signs. This is my favourite thing to teach-in my online course, Unearth Your intuition. My students already come to me being aware of 11:11 (It's not make a wish!) and have seen them many times before, but usually pass them off to just coincidence. All number sequences that show up on your phone, license plates, billboard, receipts and more, have a specific meaning and message the Universe is trying to convey to you.

111- Keep your thoughts positive.

Have you been feeling down or worried about something? 111 will usually pop up around when you are thinking low-vibe or negative thoughts. It is the most common sequence the Angels use to grab your attention. Everyone has seen or heard of it and it's misconceived meaning. As I type this, it's seriously 11:11. I wish I could show you! (Again, no such thing as coincidence!) I must be worried about how I will ever finish this book. They're right. I am. See? I need to stop that and change it to a positive. Ok: I AM FINISHED MY BOOK AND EVERYONE WHO READS IT LOVES IT. How's that? Better. Next time you see 111, please notice your thoughts and try to up level your current vibe to a more positive one because thoughts are things.

222-Your Angels are with you.

I love this one and I see it a lot. Have you ever been in a situation where you were almost in an accident, but somehow managed to swerve just in time, only to look at your clock and see 222? This happened to one of my Unearth students! She totally believes me and all the things I teach her after this frightening experience. The good news is she is ok and immediately saw 222 just before the near accident. When you see this number, I hope you remember your Angels are watching over you and protecting you.

333- The Ascended Masters.

This one packs a powerful spiritual punch and carries a valuable message. Who are the Ascended Masters? Jesus, Mary, Buddha, the Archangels, and more are believed to be Spiritually enlightened beings who were of this Earth and initiated into a higher realm of lightworkers. Their energies are the most powerful helpers we have close to us on Earth. You will typically see 333 when you are in a deep spiritual transformation or awakening, going through major life changes and upheaval. Their energies are the highest vibration possible who walk closely with us, because they have once been of this Earth as well.

444- All is well.

Phew! I'm always so grateful to see 444. I usually see this one on a license plate right when I need it. It means everything is ok and will be. Stop worrying about the little things and focus on the good.

555- A major life change is upon you.

This one is good!! They're all good though, as Spirit will never tell you anything scary or negative. Some of the 555's I have received are when we are thinking of moving, a new job is on the horizon, new opportunities, abundance, and all for the highest and best for you. Remember, the Universe loves you SO much that it's willing to shake things up a little to make your life even better. Or maybe you just deserve something amazing and this major change will show you just how deserving and special you are.

666- Turn your focus off material goods and focus on service.

Shopping a little much? Worried about finances and where the money you need will show up? This number is not negative.

It just reminds you to take your focus off material needs because the Universe is always supporting you, no matter what. Money is simply energy and energy is all around us. You are always abundant.

777- You have nothing to fear.

When you are afraid or nervous, 777 may show up right in your face. Sometimes literally. Like that license plate on the car that just drove past me now. It reminds us we really don't need to be fear- based in our thinking. Replace fear with love and you will win every time.

888- Instant manifestation.

What you've been asking for is here! This the sign of abundance and manifestation. Remember the story of the one hundred scooters at Niagara Falls? I instantly manifested the book deal and the phone call and 888 showed up 100 times! Every thought you think and word you speak is transmitted through vibration out into the Universe and is thus reflected to you; positively or negatively.

So, think positive!

999- A major chapter in your life is ending.

Again, this message is one of love and usually shows up when you are about to quit or resign from your teaching position (Wait! That's me!) or when a relationship is ending. Basically, an ending is near, but you usually will know what it is. Not usually a surprise, 999 means a chapter is ending and it's time for something new and better.

000 - A Chapter has come full circle.

After 999, you will most likely see 000. This means the previous chapter has now come full circle and has run its course and purpose for your life. When one door closes another one opens. The lesson has been learned and you are free to move on to other projects or relationship.

Notice More and You Will Receive More

Now that you are noticing all the signs motioned in this important chapter, here's something else you may like to know. Spirt has noticed you noticing. Consciously making the effort to notice these magical signs signifies to the Universe you are ready to receive an abundance of messages. Ready to receive insight and guidance for your life. You basically said, "Hey! This is kind of cool, I'd like more of those please and thank you!" Not only does verbally speaking it helps, but the physical act of you turning your head, pointing to the repeating numbers, taking photos of them, turning up the song on the radio they sent is the green light for Spirit to send more. And more is good. Trust me.

Say, for example, you see 11:11 everywhere. I start with this most common repeating number because most people are misled when noticing this one. I hate to break the news to you, but it is not "make a wish." Every time I hear someone say, "It's eleven-eleven, make a wish!" I want to reach over and smack them. It's not their fault. They have always heard others say that and it's what they may believe as well. There is nothing wrong with making a wish because it's basically asking the Universe for something positive and we could all use more of that please!

1111 really means to keep your thoughts positive. We can all be negative sometimes. When we realize how powerful our thoughts really are, changing them is beneficial for our well-being and for an amazing positive life. So, when you catch yourself thinking "Oh, my life sucks right now", stop yourself especially if 111 pops up. You will just receive more suckage. This is all explained in Chapter 7, The Law of Attraction (LOA). I could write an entire book about the LOA, because of all the detail. Manifesting our best life is all a thought away. 1111 reminds us to turn our negative thoughts around for it. Whatever we are thinking comes back to us instantly.

What types of signs do you notice the most or have you been noticing them? I am sure you are aware signs exist, but you now realize you can use them to navigate your way along this new path. Increased signs equal more guidance and magic for you. Let Spirit know you are ready for more by saying a big fat YES to them. Acknowledge, ask, seek, wish, have faith in them. They are all around you. Take photos. Post them on your wall. Spirit sees everything and knows all. They will know you're ready and willing to have it all. You just need to be open, excited, and thrilled all at the same time. Ask and more will come to you. Don't believe me? Try it for yourself.

Try it now:

Ask Spirit for a three-digit repeating number to appear today. The Universe likes to specify so you can ask for any numbers such as 333 or 555 to appear. The more you believe it will manifest, the quicker it will come.

BUT wait! There's more!

How can there be more? There is! SO much more. This is what I teach in Unearth Your Intuition. The foundation of Spirit is here for you to discover and I don't want to overwhelm you. We are just beginning to climb the spiritual ladder and like with every ladder, you don't step on the first rung and then skip over all the other rungs. That's not how ladders work. Its purpose is for climbing. This book works the same way. One step, then another and another. Until you get to the top!

Even I am not sure if there's a top to this ladder. The Universe is infinite and limitless, so there can't be a top. But you get what I mean.

The signs become more frequent and will change over time. Once you've mastered the foundation, you will start to become more curious about what else is out there. I don't mean aliens, because I have two major fears: clowns and aliens. No, thank you to both! What I am hinting at is not scary at all:

- There are more complex angel numbers such as 808, 007, 533. All numbers have specific meanings and messages.
- Words and phrases as messages. UR1DAY, POPPALUV, FLYGURL, SLDWNJEN are just a few of the ones I have received. All of course, pertain and make total sense for my life and current themes. They all arrive at the perfect time.
- Manifesting to new heights. We haven't gotten to this chapter yet, but manifesting things will become easy-peasy to you.
- Calling in Archangels such as Archangel Michael and Raphael to clear your fears and for clarity.
- Mediumistic abilities will be amped up and you could choose to pursue a similar career that helps so many people.

But I get it. It's early yet. Baby steps. Climb the ladder one rung at a time.

There's time for all this later.

CHAPTER SIX

GRATITUDE

"The greatest discovery of all time is that a person can change his future by merely changing his attitude."
-Oprah

Stop Complaining About Your Life

ONE OF THE most profound challenges I give my students is to make a list of fifty things they are grateful right this minute. Sounds easy or difficult? Depends how you look at it. In all honesty, it really should be so easy to think of fifty things to be thankful for right in this very moment. Hopefully, you are one of those people who find it easy. But that isn't always the case.

I have met so many who find it difficult to be consciously grateful for all they have. They wear their fear glasses and see the glass as half empty instead of overflowing. We have all been guilty of this. Even though we are souls having a human experience, we are in fact human with human emotions, thoughts, and sometimes things happen out of our control. We've all complained about our bosses to be d-words, a-words and sometimes mother-f words.

Our jobs can suck, we don't have enough money, we are being evicted, and someone cut us off in the grocery store line and almost took out our shin. Yes, these are all bummers, but the key here is in how we respond to it.

Complaining leads to more yuck. Grumbling leads to more things to grumble about. Thinking about how crap your day was brings you more crap. Sometimes literally. We don't like to feel that way, but sometimes it can't be helped. The key is to feel it, let the yuck surface and then let it go. Replace it with a more warm and fuzzy feeling. Stuffing it down would be worse than complaining, so let's feel it to heal it! And then, when you're feeling ok and done sitting in victim mode, ask yourself this: What was that trying to teach or show me? If you can look at it from a learning experience, you'll be better able to turn it into a positive and keep going with gratitude.

The reason gratitude is so important is because if you aren't grateful for what you already have, what makes you think you'd be happy with more? Being in a constant state of gratitude is like a magnet for more awesomeness. It's like a big ole' "Thanks, Big U, for that cool stuff I asked for!" There are so much more than fifty things to be grateful for. Why not go for a hundred or even a thousand things? Think about this the next time you start to complain about that jerk who yelled at your dog. Instead of being mad, turn it around and send that guy some love, kind of like a big Care Bear stare. Hey, it's been awhile since I used an 80's reference. I was overdue!

Next, we need to talk about the *why* in more detail. Of giving gratitude and eventually working toward having a daily practice of lists upon lists of this golden goodness. One day, you'll look back and have SO much proof that the Universe has your back you'll want to keep expressing it forever!

WHY?

I really AM going somewhere with this, I swear. As I type, I realize most of this book is leading up to the Law of Attraction. Maybe I should follow my gut and write that for the next one ☺

If we want to co-create with Spirit, and you already have been since forever, we always need to know our "why" for what we are manifesting. Why should we be grateful? Why does it matter if I make a list and check it twice? Wait, that's Santa's list. Hold on. Most important, the what and why we are grateful is the best way to find our way to happy. We can't be sad when we are grateful. We are too busy celebrating all this cool and miraculous stuff! Things like: our bed, pillows, running hot water, tea, my jammies, my family....Mine again, but I bet your list would resemble mine too.

If your why is for material gain or has an underlying neediness/ greediness to it, you can fuhgeddaboudit. Not that you would, but it's been done before. Think of your "why" as how it can help, improve, enhance your well-being. Let's use my manifestation process for my new home.

We really wanted to move into a bigger, much more updated, and beautiful home. I could visualize it so clearly and knew we'd find the perfect house that was within our budget. At the time, I asked the Universe for a new house. Our WHY was because we had outgrown our small upper, it was getting run down, dirty, outdate and most of all, we deserved it. Remember the Universe wants you to see yourself through it's eyes. We are all superstars in the big U's eyes, even if we are unable to see it for ourselves. I knew we were "better" than a cramped place for our family of six. The "why" was because we are awesome, and it would be for our highest good and best life. Plus, the house I ended up manifesting was everything I asked for and more. My why was aligned.

If, on the other hand, I had wanted the big house in the fancy neighbourhood because I wanted to raise my social status, show off, and throw big parties, or just because I felt like it, the Universe most likely wouldn't have delivered. It may have had way more bumps and obstacles thrown in our way. The why would have been for the "wrong" reasons. Wanting to look good to others is not a good why. I don't even like to throw parties. As it turns out my neighbours drive fancy cars and I do not. That's ok. Their "why" is different.

When we did manifest our home (just how I envisioned it), we were over the moon. Updated, bigger, and more suited for our growing family. We have space, the kids have their own room and we no longer have a dirty carpet. Hardwood. This is not in a braggy ha-ha sucks to be you story, but to show you that if I can manifest the home we asked the Universe for, so can you. If your intention is for the best. And when we finally got the keys, you can be your sweet hinny we said, "OMG THANK YOU SO MUCH! IT'S PERFECT." I may have kissed the front door. And…um…the hardwood. Ok fine, I kissed the stainless-steel fridge. You didn't live with an ugly old dirty white fridge for 8 years. ☺

Thank you Schmank you

As mentioned earlier, when someone gives you a present or what you asked for, in human form, you say thank you! You appreciate the delivery (wrapping), the gas money they paid to drive to your house, the effort behind their choice. When the UNIVERSE delivers the goods, you gotta say thank you! Thank you and being grateful is an amplifier. It says to the Universe, "I love what you brought me and it's so special I would like some more of that goodness. Thank you very much. Please and thank you." The Universe goes, "Oh wow she's super thankful for all of the goodness I sent her way. That makes me feel appreciated so I'm going to give her some more cool stuff!!" See how that works? Saying thank you and taking a moment to really feel and appreciate the manifestation only takes a second or two and very little effort. Want more of the good? Take a second.

Remember that when you express gratitude for your gifts, it's important to feeeeeeeeeel the love. Like really feel it in your heart. I'm not talking about saying "Um, ya. Thanks man. See ya later. Have a nice day" and scoff it off. You really need to sense the emotion behind it. Don't forget, this was something you really wanted which brought you joy! Joy is like another type of amplifier and magnet as well. Why do I keep talking about law of attraction in here? Because it fits. It makes sense. It's setting the stage for the next chapter. Hopefully I don't repeat myself too much. As you can probably guess, I haven't written it yet. It's totally stressing me out. Like I want to skip to Chapter Nine because it's fun.

I think you get it. You get a gift, you say thank you. You get a new house, you feel happy. You manifested a big fat check just in time, you do a jig or some other form of body movement. I know I sure would. Someone has big dreams to travel to Bali and a big fat check would be fantastic. Do you hear that universe? BIG and FAT and lots of zeros. See my why for Bali isn't for greed and I'm trusting it will arrive when I'm meant to go there. I have such big dreams for working there, helping others, being on a team of amazing people. My why is cool and it will allow me to serve others. My why and my saying thank you for it already being here even though it's not is what keeps moving it toward me. So, thank you, thank you, thank you, thank you, thank you, I love you, thank you. You get the idea.

Try it and see what happens. Walk around being joyful and grateful all the time if you can. There really is so much to be grateful for in all our lives. It doesn't matter if you're ill, losing friends, your hamster Petey died. There is always something to be grateful for. I bet you're super grateful right now for this cool book. ☺

Open Your Eyes to Abundance

I am grateful to YOU for buying this book and reading it! I am grateful for the people who helped me work on this book, the program, the ones who worked behind the scenes, the publisher, the editor and formatter, and the people who were with me when this entire program and idea gave birth.

We are all abundant beings. The Universe is entirely made up of abundance which can mean different things to different people. It doesn't always mean cold hard cash. Although who doesn't love money? I DO! I'd marry it if I could.

Abundance is well, abundant. It's everywhere. It's like a source of constant flowing water we can tap into at will. Creativity, opportunities, helpful people, resources, ideas and yes, money. It's in everything and is everywhere. Since the big U is all about abundance and you are part of the Universe, that means YOU are abundant too. The only issue is that some of us don't believe we are worthy or know how to tap into it.

It is the force that makes the grass grow, the trees stand tall and sway, the sun know to shine, how water flows in a river, stones, birds, air, resources, friends, people, money. It's all around you. Take a minute and put your hand on your heart and feel that. That is an abundance of love. You've got it. It's in you too.

The next time you are going for a walk, look around you. Is there enough sidewalk for you to walk on? Are there fields around you? How do you feel about that? Marvel in the miracles. If you don't think the Universe and you are miracles, you're missing the point of living!

I bet you can guess the one way to tap in to abundance. Yes, that's right, GRATITUDE! I know you're probably thinking: "THAT'S IT? THIS CHICK IS TELLING ME ALL I HAVE TO DO IS SAY THANK YOU FOR SOMETHING AND I WILL GET MORE OF IT??" I'm not crazy, I swear. Being grateful is like a big magnet. The other important part is to realize that a) you are abundant, b) you are worthy of it (yes, you are!) and c) how to access it.

Repeat after me:

> I AM ABUNDANT AS FUK% (Yes, I swore)
> THERE IS MORE THAN ENOUGH FOR EVERYONE. ENOUGH MONEY.
> ENOUGH TIME.
> ENOUGH LOVE.
> ENOUGH MONEY. (some struggle with this truth)
> SO MUCH ABUNDANCE.

Making A List

The easiest way to feel abundant and gratitude is to make a list. Lists are concrete proof and remind us that we have so much to be thankful for. Even when things get thrown in the crapper. By making a list and sitting for a few minutes with ourselves, you will see how easily gratitude can flow right out of you.

One of the many challenges I give my participants in the program is to construct a gratitude list of at least fifty things they are grateful in that moment. Sometimes I push them to come up with one hundred things. It doesn't matter if things are going swimmingly in their lives or badly. The whole point of this exercise is to see how abundant we already are. We don't thank the Universe for what we want, we thank it for what we ALREADY HAVE. Because if you aren't happy and full of joy for all the amazing things you *already* have, what makes you think you would be happy with more? No matter if you ask for it or not, remember the Universe loves you and wants you to be happy. Joy attracts more joy.

Here is what you can do to start using the magnetic powers of gratitude:

Paper and pen in hand, write the numbers 1- 50 on the page. As your heart comes up with all the things you are grateful for, I want you to feel it in your body. Feeling gratitude amplifies it but take note: you can't trick or fool the Universe. You can't pretend to be grateful. It doesn't work that way; it'll see right through you. Take a deep breath and go for it! If you get stuck, look around your room or wherever you are compiling your list. In your bedroom? Express a deep heart-felt thank you for your bed, the duvet you cuddle in, the lamp to see, the door to close that gives you a break from the kids, or your never-ending work. Once it starts a- flowing, there ain't no stopping this list from growing. If you're at the kitchen table, say thank you for your running water, the kettle, the food, the cupboards, and the stove! Hey, with no stove you could get tired of microwave dinners quick!

Make your list now. I will wait.

How many things came easily? Was it a bit tricky toward the end or did the gratitude just flow right out of you? Someday it may be harder to do and some days, the sun shines so bright you gotta wear shades. Normal. Some days, I can rhyme off a hundred things I am thankful for and on "*those*" days, it's a struggle or I don't do it at all. But let me tell you, those are the times when you really need to make the list.

When things are going downhill, the best way to get back up is to list *everything* and anything you can think of to be grateful for. Even if it's only the air you breathe or that you have a face. Dude, there is always, always, something to be grateful for, especially when things are low and you're on the ground. Just even thinking about how you have hands or a mind that comprehends what is happening can make you stop for a second and come back to present. Those days may even become less and less rude and frequent visitors. Your entire attitude and mood can come back to joy in a matter of seconds. Just remember that our natural state of being is JOY!

So, make that list.

You will be so thankful you did.

Forever and Ever

One of the questions I receive from my students is, "*How long do I have to do this for?*" when referring to making the gratitude list. My answer is, "FOREVA and EVA!" Does that answer your question? Why wouldn't you make this a lifelong habit? Do it for a week and watch how you feel whenever you look around you or that car cut you off on the highway. Notice how you feel now. You'll be surprised what a little gratitude can do for not only you, but those around you!

It doesn't take long to sit. Have a tea. Breathe. Take time for you. Five minutes is all it should take, unless you're feeling SUPER grateful that day! Then by all means, go for it and go longer. The dishes can wait, the kids can wipe their own noses, and the dog can let himself out this one time. The more you do this, the better you will feel. Here's a crazy idea: **Why not make it part of your morning routine?**

What if instead of immediately grabbing your phone when you woke up, you grabbed your list and a pen?

Would you freak out and have a mini heart attack if you changed it up just a teensy-weensy bit?

What if you reached for your gratitude journal just this once?

Imagine waking up and not feeling lack from seeing the awesome vacations your friends are taking without you as you scroll through Facebook. Instead you could feel joy and happiness first thing. Heck, why don't you even throw in a five-minute meditation? It really is the little things that make us feel happy.

Don't believe me? I triple dog dare you to try this tomorrow morning.

Because who doesn't want to wake up smiling? I know you do. Just a small shift can change everything. If you want to keep scrolling Social Media first thing, go for it. I am guilty of it too. I just prefer my list and meditation.

Gratitude attracts more things to be grateful for. Joy attracts more joy. It only takes thirty-days to form a solid routine. We can do this for that long. Maybe even longer. Maybe even for the rest of our lives, because there really is so much to say thank you for. Even that sweater you didn't like that you got for your birthday. Maybe you can learn to love it. Fall days are cold ☺

The next chapter is what I like to call the ***doozy*** chapter. The motherload of all chapters. The one I have been referring to this entire book so far. Everything will make sense shortly. As soon as you turn the page. You know you want to look. It's time to buckle down and get to work.

"When things are going downhill, the best way to get back up is to list everything and anything you can think of to be grateful for.

Even if it's only the air you breathe or that you have a face."

CHAPTER SEVEN

THE LAW OF ATTRACTION 101

"There is nothing you cannot be or do or have."
-Abraham Hicks

Law of Attraction 101

HERE COMES THE science-y part!

The Law of Attraction is the attractive, magnetic power of the Universe that draws similar energies together. It manifests through the power of creation, everywhere and in many ways. Even the law of gravity is part of the law of attraction. This law attracts thoughts, ideas, people, situations, and circumstances.

Powerful stuff, isn't it?

You can think of the LOA (*I'm going to refer to it as this from now on)* as two powerful magnets between you and the big U. Start to visualize a big fat magnet from your head and another one that is attached to the Universal energy. This powerful magnetic force goes back and forth between the two of you constantly.

Your thoughts, emotions, words (spoken and written) are vibrations that are always being transmitted into the Universe. Every. Single. Thought. Positive or negative. Whatever you put out is what you will naturally receive back. This is where the saying, like attracts like fits perfectly. Let's say for example, you have the constant thought: "MY LIFE IS CRAP!" (Not me, Universe! I am just using this as an example for my reader Doesn't count I don't really mean it!)

If you say that out loud in a discussion with a co-worker or even text it to your boyfriend, you can expect some more crapola in return within a very short time. IMPORTANT NOTE: The Universe does *not* punish anyone; it simply RESPONDS to your vibration. Cool?

Keeping with the crapola theme, when your thoughts and feelings are a powerful vibration that gets shot out into the big U, the Big U goes, "Oh ok! You like the crap? Here is some more crap." Not in a jerk kind of way. Just in a responding to your mood kinda way.

You can guess what would happen if you said," OHMYGOD, Becky, look at her butt!" Wait, what? No, wrong example. If you said, "WOW! My life is amazing. I am so full of joy!" and you felt it and believed it, the Universe would respond with, "You got it dude!" and shoot you some more thumbs up.

I know, I know, it's ok. It's a tad overwhelming. If I'm being one hundred percent honest, it took me TWO YEARS to totally grasp this concept. I read a million-ish books about it. This was the book that landed on my lap that day at my friend's house that day I had asked for a sign. We can do this. Together.

I've Got the Feels

When you ask or request something for you highest and best from the Universe, there is another key element that goes into making it happen.

Let's review:

- You need to ask specifically for what you want (put your order in in Amazon or Sears).
- Trust it will come (put it in the cart)
- Wait for it to arrive on your doorstep (your life)

If you want to amplify the vibration going outward into the great beyond, not only do you need to say thank you in advance, but you've got to FEEL your way to it.

Here is the perfect way to manifest your dream with feeling:

I like to do videos of me acting out the scene of what I am trying to manifest. This is going to sound ridiculous but let me assure, it works like a charm. I have manifested $10,000 and a trip by doing this extremely powerful method of manifestation.

I wanted to manifest a trip to Disney World. Yes, that IS my dream vacay and I will be going. So, I put up my iPhone on the dresser, got out my suitcase (which was empty), made up a fake check for $10,000 and really got in the momentum of what it would feel like if I already had these things and that I was getting ready to take my kids there. With FEELING, I said aloud and acted my little heart out:

"*OMG you guys, I am so excited because I have Just packed my suitcase for Disney world! We haven't told the kids yet, but we will tomorrow morning which is CHRISTMAS morning!! No present this year because this trip is their gift! EEEEEKKK I cannot wait! There is no way I am going to be sleeping tonight!! We have all their passports ready to go, their bags are packed, and we leave tomorrow early. My parents are driving us in their SUV and they will be so surprised, I am* *so going to video their faces when we tell them!! Also, I just got this big fat check or $10,000 to pay for the trip and first-class seats so we don't ever have to worry about money the entire time. Everything is paid for! We have the best hotel and we are going to have the best memories for this once in lifetime trip to my ultimate destination dream: DISNEY!!"*

Don't forget I said that you cannot trick the universe. You can imagine how much I felt the emotions in his video that day. I almost teared up because I got so into how I would feel as if it had already happened for me. For those who know me, Disney is my only dream vacation. I don't care if I travel to Cuba, Dominican. Take me straight to the Tigger express. Is that even a thing? I wouldn't know, I've never been there. But I AM! I wasn't tricking the Universe. All those emotions and words were real in the moment and that is what will bring me the trip. I don't know how it's going to come about, but I know without a doubt that it will. I don't need to worry about the how. That's the Universe's job. My job is to feel it and believe it is on it's way to me!

Author's note: I have also manifested the trip to Disney. I got to go with my daughter in May 2018.

Let it Go

Speaking of Disney, can't you just hear Elsa belting out the tune, Let It Go? It's the perfect song to explain another key element and component to making the LOA work for you. Letting go, or what I like to call it, surrender, is paramount. (PS. I forgot to mention that I did manifest that big fat check for $10,000. That check allowed me to resign from my job and live on it until my business started taking off. I was so grateful for that money. I had no idea how I would ever be able to receive it, but I asked, I trusted, and I let go. Then bam. Here is ten grand for you to be ok after quitting your job with no parachute! See how that works?)

Letting go of the *how* allows the universe to- do its thang. If you are worrying about how it will come, it won't. Holding on tightly for dear life to the possible outcomes only *repels* the thing from manifesting. Surrender to the big U. Allow it to do its job. Then you do yours by handing it over fully and fill your entire being full of faith. After all, Amazon always delivers so why wouldn't the Universe?

Surrendering also shows the Universe that you are trusting one hundred percent in its abilities to deliver. Give the Universe some wiggle room and stop following it around like a puppy. Give it the freedom it needs to show you how it gets things done. Can you imagine walking round everywhere hanging on to your significant others arm all day long because you don't trust them to go anywhere on their own or around the grocery store pulling on their leg to make sure they choose the right groceries? It would be exhausting to do that. You trust that they can do the groceries or going for a walk without your help. At least I sure hope so! Give them the freedom to bring you what you need on its terms. Don't worry about the how. They may do it differently than you but that's ok. We all get the same result.

Also, the how is not important. Who cares how your request manifests? Trust that is already on its way and coming to you soon. It may not show up the way you imagined but the Big U is also very clever and has a sense of humour. Asking for $2000 for a vacay? Maybe your Grandma gives you a big fat check unexpectedly! That is so not what you expected or how you imagined it would come to fruition. You asked and here it is Take it and then say thank you. To your Grandma, too.

Do You Believe in Magic?

Have you heard the saying "I'll believe it when I see it?" I'm going to be straight up with you and tell you. That's total bullshit and not how the LOA works. Instead, imagine a world where you said, "I'll SEE it WHEN I believe it!" Doesn't that feel better?

You've probably heard that saying a million times in the great span of your life up to this point. We all have these beliefs that have been instilled and stamped into our subconscious since forever. When we were born, we were like a clean piece of paper that screamed and pooped. We didn't have any qualms about our noses or any beliefs at all. Fresh and clean Buttttt then, Mom and Dad, friends, siblings school teachers, and society told us that we need proof if something is to be considered "real" or to believe it. "Back to reality" is a popular one after a vacation or long weekend. It's so funny to me how this isn't truth either. Reality is what we make it. We can manifest any life we wish. Happy life, happy job, joy, abundance, a big home, car, money, friends and more! ***All we have to do is ask.***

The tricky part is we must believe. I know, I know. We were taught believing is hard to do. We've all been told seeing is believing, but what if I told you it's the opposite? Because well, um it is. Faith and trust must be our core feelings. If we don't believe we are deserving of the thing, whatever the thing is, it's going to either not manifest or take a reeeaaally long time.

Take a leap of faith in the Universe. Believe BEFORE you see it. Be so rooted in your faith that it can't help but manifest right before your eyes. Believing is seeing. That is where the magic happens.

Manifestation *is* magic. Once you get the hang of the LOA, you can make anything you want to appear.

If you have:

- the asking
- trust
- surrender
- action
- complete faith

ABRACADABRA. Your friends will start calling you Harry. Harry Potter, that is. Wield your magic elder wand and make it happen. That is how powerful you are when you co-create with Spirit. I have an idea. Let's try our magic out, shall we? Close your eyes. Go ahead. Wait, how can you read if your eyes are closed?

Ok, read first, then close your eyes. Ask Spirit for a feather or a dime. Feel it in your being that you know without a doubt it will be delivered to you. Don't worry about how it will manifest, just ask. Now surrender the how and wait. Be patient. Don't strangle it by worrying about when it will come or become impatient. The more you believe it's already on it's way, the quicker it will arrive. It can be an actual feather, a picture of a feather, someone says the word feather. It doesn't mater. Remember Spirit has a sense of humour but also loves you so much it wants to see you happy. When you get your feather, take a photo.

You will get one. You're welcome.

Don't Stop Believing

Now that you hopefully realize how magical and powerful you have always been, what will you do to keep this feeling going, well, forever? Because this magic in you isn't a one-time deal. Once you've mastered all the steps, you can have all the things. All the things have always been there. You just weren't sure how to tap into it. Abundance is yours. It will be like a constant ever-flowing tap of everything you need. Just don't stop believing. I love that song. Thanks, Journey. This is one of the songs that Spirit sends me when my faith is shaking.

Going forward from here, you may lose your momentum once in a while or you may lose faith when something goes wrong. Don't worry. You can always come back to this chapter later to remind yourself of the necessary steps and how you manifested that incredible thing. Believe that Spirit has your back. Believe that you are being heard and that Spirit knows everything you say, think, or feel. Believe that you are on the best path possible when you are trusting in Source and have so much faith inside you that you can feel it seeping out of your heart. Allow it to flow. Allow it to come to you. If you can hold it in your mind, you can hold it in your hand.

What if You Do Stop Believing?

What if you forget everything I've said to you in this book? What if you don't get the feather, dime, or money that you asked for? Are you really noticing the signs that it's on its way? Did you ignore that person's help or that idea you had? Be open. Like really open to all the Universal offerings, because there's so much help available to you. It's everywhere.

Keep your eyes open when you go for a walk or a drive. Believe that the feather on the ground is for you and not from a bird. Again, I don't want to make you do anything, but you wouldn't have read this chapter if you didn't already have some sort of faith in the unknown and invisible. Heck, you wouldn't have bought this book at all! You do believe in something. You do believe it's possible to have the life you deserve. Believe you are worthy of all of it. Because you are. Yes, you. The one reading in her pjs. I am so jealous right now. I want my pjs. I think I'm going to manifest some new ones. Oh, the Big U just heard that. In no time flat, I will have new ones. Cute flannel ones that are plaid with buttons down the front. You can bet your ass those pjs are mine. How do I know? Because I BELIEVE!! When you believe it, you will see it.DO not hold back for one second.

I really feel that it's important to tell you something even though I don't know you personally. Except for my Mom. And my sister. Hi guys! Even if I don't know you, there IS something

I do know about you. And that is you are incredible. Amazing. Worthy. Fun. Beautiful. Abundant. Hot stuff. And a lot of other words that describe you. Yes, you. You're amazing for wanting to remember how to use your superpowers. You are amazing for having the courage to buy this cool book for yourself and for making a tea for your quiet time alone. You are so abundant, you don't even know it. Yet. You will.

But don't let a stranger (me) tell you that. You've got to believe it for yourself. When you see your worth as the Universe does, your life will radically become more vibrant and colorful. When you believe that you are worthy of everything your heart desires, it will come. There is so much power within you, I can't even tell you how much. Well, at least I've been trying to tell you! I hope a part, if not all of you, listens. The Universe loves you unconditionally. Stop being so hard on yourself. Stop beating yourself up for not doing everything perfect today. Instead, why not give some lovin' on yourself a try. It feels way better and it's how it is supposed to be.

You are an intricate part of the Universe. You wouldn't be here if you weren't needed or loved times infinity. You are here for a very important reason and believing you aren't special is counterproductive. The Universe is like, "DUDE, see me as I see you." See yourself through the eyes of the most powerful force and you can begin to feel it too. That is my wish for you.

Whoa, where did that sappy stuff come from? I think Spirit really wanted me to tell you that at that exact moment. It's almost like the Big U knew you needed to hear and read those words at this exact moment. I was supposed to write something else here, but I changed my mind. Everyone is allowed to change their mind, even if they committed to something else. I hope I didn't disappoint you by changing this part of the book. I think it was about not holding back. So, don't hold back. There. I said it. 'Nuff said.

In the next chapter, we will chat about your superpowers on steroids, if you choose to go there. To the next level that is. Not steroids. Those are bad for you. And you should totally go to the next chapter. Choose to go there. It's awesome. See you in a minute.

CHAPTER EIGHT

THE CLAIR'S

"Close both eyes to see with the other."-Rumi

The Clair's

CLAIR SIMPLY PUT, means clear. There are 5 main Clair's that are used to describe one's abilities in using not only their intuition, but also in communicating with Spirit. Say for example, you are driving along the highway and Siri says to turn left on a small sideroad. While I trust her maybe 90 percent of the time, remember you do have your own inner GPS system at work. If it's a trip you have done once before, you may choose to use your inner knowing (Claicognizance) and choose to ignore Siri's suggestion. You may feel like you know how to get there from memory and feeling. If all else fails and you get lost, you can go back to Siri. ☺

When we communicate with Spirit (and you have been doing this already when you asked for the feather or a sign-asking, verbal or mental, is in fact communication, don't freak out) what we ultimately want it to receive or get the answers in a clear way.

Who wants fuzzy answers that we must decipher a code? Not this gal. By using clear ways to send and receive messages (intuitive), we ultimately want them to be clear and that is where the word Clair comes in. Why didn't they just use the word, clear, anyway? It would make things so much simpler.

The five clairs are like our five senses: hear, smell, touch, taste, and sight. Just the same way we communicate and survive in the human world, we can use these five senses to navigate the spirit world and universal energies. Spirit is everywhere, so I don't want you to panic when I talk about communicating with it. You have been doing so since forever. You don't have to speak to loved ones who have passed over like I do. Or maybe you're extremely interested in mediumship and not freaking out. Whichever way you are at this moment, just realize your intuition will grow from here on out and anything is possible for you. If a former kindergarten teacher and "regular" mom of four kids can quit her job to communicate with Spirit full-time, you can see where I am going with this

Just likc your senses, Clair's only function properly when they are working clearly and efficiently. And usually you aren't using them all at the same time. Same goes for your abilities. One will be stronger than others, but sometimes you may use them all at once.

Think about being at a fair. The senses you probably use the most are hearing and smell— mmmmmm cotton candy. You already know you're at the fair. You hear the rides, the screaming kids and long for earplugs. Unless it's your own kids then that wouldn't look very good. You can smell the hotdogs and candy apples a mile away and if your fair is in the country, you probably smell the cows and horses as well. The sounds and smells are so clear, you don't need to tweak anything to revive them. You're good.

Same as when you're using your superpowers. They will need to be clear. One or two of your powers will be stronger and used more than the others depending on where you are (fair) and what you are experience (loud sounds and cotton candy). Which ones you use the most will become more evident to you over time and with practice. Why don't we figure out which ones after I lay them all out for you?

Clairvoyance

This is probably the most common Clair of them all. It translates to clear-seeing. By seeing, it isn't always physical seeing with our two eyes. Clairvoyance is usually seeing in your mind's eye. Some Mediums can see Spirit in physical form while I prefer to see them in my mind's eye as if they were standing there beside me. I have never seen a Spirit with my physical eyes, but I do see them with my mind, which is just fine with me. Seeing Spirit, a loved one who has passed, can be frightening and might make the Medium or intuitive fearful enough to give up their gifts. And we don't want that.

Clairvoyance can also aid in using your superpowers. Let's say you wake up at 5 am ready for the work day and all of a sudden in your mind's eye you see a tire on an angle as if it is being lifted by a tow truck. You can probably guess this is my personal example. You see it clear as anything and you feel like it may mean something, but you brush it off, jump in the shower, and then the van anyway, hoping it was just a fluke or your imagination. You drive to work and everything you saw in your mind' eye (clairvoyantly) happens. Your van breaks down after being pulled over by an officer for other reasons and then gets towed by a tow truck driver. Yes, true story, but a perfect example of how clear seeing is a strong ability, whether you ignore it or not. I totally would have gone to work regardless of the day's unfolding events. Seeing the image of the tire on an angle as if being towed totally made sense to me later that day.

If you're a Medium or want to pursue Mediumship courses to further your development and your intuition to a very exciting level, you will notice clairvoyance is super helpful when doing readings. Usually it starts off as a fuzzy image and it is difficult to make out a loved one's appearance. With practice and strengthen this Clair, eventually the images or visions will become clearer. Think of going to the optometrist when they put on that contraption over your eyes. The doctor makes it fuzzy on purpose and then switches it to clear seeing. It would be nice if it was this quick to be clairvoyant! But alas, we must work on our abilities daily and over time, we will see that big fat "E" on the board. I mean Spirit.

The images in your mind's eye can become clearer with practice and time. Some may see images like a movie in their mind. This isn't your imagination. This is your ability working to help communicate with Spirit. I told you you'd have superpowers. ☺ Some see colours, images, or visions on the screen of their mind. These hold vital intuitive meaning for us. Do not discount what you see in your mind now that you are aware of your amazing abilities. This is Spirit in action talking to you!

Don't worry if you're not seeing anything at first. I'm willing to bet you may be more apt in one of the other four clairs! Ooooooh maybe you hear the information! Let's see.

Clairaudience

Can you guess which sense/ability this is? Yep, you got it. Clear hearing. This is my personal favourite Clair and I use this one the most as a Medium.

There are two ways to "hear" information from Spirit: as a voice in your head OR a physical literal voice. Now, personally, I prefer the one in my head. It is more common to hear Spirit this way although if you're brave, you can ask Spirit to speak to you aloud. Me? No, thank you very much. Of course, I have an example of when you ask Spirit to speak to you aloud you get it. And then you freak out and tell Spirit no effing way. We are so done with that.

In the early stages of my Mediumship/intuitive development, my teacher told me that my clairaudience would be grow and come through strong and clear shortly. I had no idea that her image of corn growing out of my ears (right?) would be so profound. Being saucy that I am, I decided to test the waters and ask Spirit (specifically my grandmother) to speak to me aloud. I didn't mean at the grocery store parking lot. But that's what she did. Great timing, Grandma. As I war pushing full cart of food to my car, I CLEARLY heard her voice, yelling out my name, "Jennifer." I actually turned around expecting to see her standing there. Of course, I didn't see her (clairvoyance is not my forte), but I knew it was her voice. I totally panicked and freak out and said very firmly, "NO MORE." I don't know why I was so afraid because a) I had asked to hear it physically and b) a grocery store parking lot? Seriously? I think I was just surprised at how CLEAR it was! Like she was just, well, there.

Hearing it in your mind is a lot less intimidating, although it can be difficult to decipher if what you are hearing is your own voice or that of Spirit. Again, with time and practice, you can begin to figure out which is which. Trust is key in this case as well. You can go around thinking, "Oh that is just my inner voice saying those things." Nope. Spirit communicates this way as well and that includes our Spirit Guides, Angels, and Loved O in Spirit ones. Our team sometimes speaks or attempts to give us important information this way as well. Learning how to decipher the differences in tones and voices is an amazing way to communicate with Spirit. I think it might just be my favourite. Ok fine, it's my favourite because it's my strongest Clair. Clairaudience is like my favourite subject in school because I was good at it and it was fun. Clairvoyance is like math. Ugh. I wasn't good at it and it wasn't my strong suit. Heck, it wasn't any suit. And who needs math? Math schmath. You don't use it in writing books now, do you? I win.

When you hear the guidance in your day-to- day life, it may show up when you are ignoring your gut and turning down the wrong street like I did back in Chapter 3. Your Guides will sometimes yell at you. Not to hurt your feelings of course, but to help. That is their job. They don't have to yell. But mine do, because I don't always listen to them. Sometimes I like to be the one who's right. I guess I should listen more. I hear them loud and clear and over time, we will both trust our Guides more. It takes time. As I write this sentence, my Spirit Guides be like, "Shakes head." They're probably used to it.

Clairsentience

Clairsentience is clear feeling. I received this sense from day one of my practice and it comes up a lot with my *Unearth Your Intuition* students. When you meditate (you did today, right?), you are opening up to Spirit and all the energy that surrounds you constantly. You just might be too busy to notice!

With intuition, you may have felt like someone was staring at your pretty face from across the room only to look up and yep, that hot guy is ***totally*** checking you out. You might also use clairsentience to feel a group of people out and one person may make you want to run and another might make you feel happy. Always follow your inner feeling for this is important information.

But remember, your superpowers are more than just for navigating your day to day life now. You have put on the cape of wonder and have signaled to Spirit that you want more. More abundance, more information, more communication. Instead of just using it for *knowing* your way around, what if we used it for something cooler and awesome-er? That's a word, right? Well, it is now. MY superpower is making words up.

We can also use clairsentience to just feel energy around us. When you meditate, you may have felt some strange sensations around the top of your head or around your body. These are not to be feared but celebrated. You are communicating with Spirit. I used to feel all kinds of energy around me when I began my meditation practice. I would feel my head tingle, a twisting sensation in my forehead, pins and needles on my arm and even spirit energy beside me! SO COOL. This was simply my clairsentience developing and shaping. It was like Spirit was gently introducing itself to me in this way. Almost like a shy new friend who is worried it's too soon to hug you. (But we just met!) Personally, I didn't mind the sensations because I had a teacher who would answer my questions and when she did, I felt ok with it. You may not have a Mentor or teacher to guide you, but I am here to let you know what those sensations are. I've been through it and it has taken me to new heights in my meditations. It is simply Spirit giving you the thumbs up to keep going and exploring what this whole new experience is all about.

It is also important to tell you at this part in the book that you cannot make or force Spirit to give you the Clair you want to use. By that I mean if you just *know* things very strongly (claircognizant), you can't make yourself ***hear*** Spirit. Spirit wears the pants in this relationship. You can always ask to hear, like I did that day in the parking lot, but it will come when it comes. You can't put in your order to see Spirit in physical form, like, tomorrow. And would you want that? Would that be for your highest and best? Probably not. It would likely scare the crap out of you and have you quitting this journey due to fear and shock. Spirit would never do anything to scare you and only wants what is best. You are amazing and have a gift. Yes, you sure do. You've got to share it with the world. That's why you came here. Not to push papers or be sad all the time.

That's another story for another book I may write.

After I finally finish this one!

Claircognizance

Writer's note:
OK so here's the truth/deal.

I have been stuck. Like, writer's block or procrastination, self-sabotage…whatever you want to call it. I have been telling myself that I will finish it one day. I will wait until I am inspired and stuff. But today I just decided to keep going. Keep writing. I have so many people asking me, "When is your book going to come out, Jen?" and I keep pushing it off. So, today I decided that I would open my laptop, and instead of scrolling through Facebook for the millionth time, I would write. Write whatever came up. And that is what I am going to do. Or rather, what I am doing right at this very moment. Well. Not your moment as you are reading this sentence. That wouldn't make any sense.

Back to work! Let's get this book done so I can help all of you!

Claircognizance is the ability to just "know" something intuitively. It's that feeling of "something bad is going to happen" or "predicting" that your sister is pregnant because you just know. You don't know how you know, but you're very sure you're right. Most times, these things will happen and you may wonder if you're a freak or just lucky. You aren't either of those things. You are incredibly powerful!

For me, this Clair is mostly used in my Mediumship readings. Loved Ones in Spirit communicate with me via clairaudience or claircognizance. They give me confidence to express to you what they are trying to convey. Here is an example:

I was doing a large group event at a local restaurant and a brother in Spirit came forward the last reading. I KNEW he was male. I could just tell. I didn't have to rely on my clairaudience to see the color grey (which is my usual reference for a male spirit). I just knew he was a male. Claircognizance at its best!

When I was younger, I remember lying in bed in the middle of the night and waking up with a start. My whole body got tense and I just knew that the phone was about to ring. I also knew, somehow, that it would be news that my Grandmother had just had a heart attack. Sure enough, a minute later, the phone rings. I am sure you can guess what the news was. I know some of my readers are thinking to themselves, right at this moment, "Oh my god, that's happened to me so many times!" That's because you are an intuitive being and you have always been, my dear. Always. You just forgot, and it laid dormant. Not anymore!

Getting Clear on Your Strongest Clair

How do you get clear on which ability is your strongest? Well, we need to go back to the very beginning where we discussed, and you groaned, about meditation. Meditation is the key to developing every one of these clairs. Why? Because getting quiet and turning off your monkey brain is the only way you can hear, feel, and be attuned with Source energy. It does exist all around you yes, but you cannot be in alignment with it fully if you don't sit still. Don't be intimidated by getting quiet. Fifteen minutes tops. You have the time. You will make the time if you don't. If transforming and up-leveling your abilities and your life is a priority to you, then you will do it.

Practice, practice, practice will also help in clarifying which of your superpowers is top dog. The more you work on your gifts, the clearer and more accurate they will become. It's also helpful to know that once you've figured out which Clair stands out, Spirit may change it! Just when you have your clear- knowing (claircognizance) down pat, things could get all shook up and you may find another clair becomes dominant. In my Mediumship practice, my most powerful and most-used ability is clairaudience.

In the beginning of my journey, I relied on my clairsentience to feel my way, get it?

Over time, your abilities will strengthen provided you meditate consistently and practice regularly. When you meditate, you are connected to Source energy (aka Spirit) and that's the most important aspect to this work. You cannot work with Spirit if you do not show you are open to receiving, working, and growing. It IS work, but it's the most fun work I've ever known. Once you get going, you'll be able to do so much more than feeling your way when you get lost or are making decisions. You will bypass the small tasks and work your way up to the big stuff!

In the next chapter, (because you know you want to keep reading!) we will talk in more detail what the next steps will be for you! How exciting is that? Did you have any idea you would have come this far in your journey so quickly? Did you know that your inner GPS would end up being so much more than that? I bet you did, somewhere inside of you. You always knew. You always knew there was "something bigger" to this world, your life, and yourself. Congratulations! You were right all along and now you're more than ready to go forward, develop, explore, help, discover, and dream!

The Possibilities are Endless

*"This isn't your imagination.
This is your ability working to
help communicate with Spirit.
I told you you'd have
superpowers. ☺."*

CHAPTER NINE

THE POSSIBILITIES ARE ENDLESS NOW

The Next Step

NO, I'M NOT talking about your pre-teen's favorite show. This is about YOU. For YOU. It's time for you to step up and step out! Get pumped up. Get excited. Get ready for more than what you've always known. So, what do you do now? Well, that is totally up to you, but I have some ideas to help you decide:

Find Lost Objects

This is a fun way to use your superpowers and I use this exercise in my *Unearth Your Intuition* program. Have you ever lost your keys? Of course, you have! Try this the next time you lose them. All you must do is ASK. Ask spirit, "Where are my keys?"

Yes, I am totally serious. I do this all the time! You can ask in your head, or if you don't care who's listening, out loud. It works the same.

Now if you're clairaudient, you will "hear" what I like to call an "invisible" voice in your head. Do not freak out. It's a bit different than your own voice in your head. It will feel different and you are NOT going cray-cray. This is Spirit!! Once you recognize that voice as Spirit (it may feel like your imagination!) listen! Listen to that voice because it is your superpower at work.

What may happen is that Spirit will either tell you straight up where your keys are (or some other lost object like glasses) OR you will hear or see in your mind the "story" leading up to where the keys are.

Here is an example of how I found a lost ring. My favorite ring, no less. It was lost and I really wanted to wear it to an event I had that night. Before I got to the freaking out part, I sat down and closed my eyes. I took a breath and said in my head, "Where is my ring?" Immediately, I heard, "IN YOUR PURSE!" I heard it in my head, but it was definitely not my imagination. I went to check my purse and nothing. It wasn't there. So, I asked again. "Where is my ring?" Then I heard, "IN YOUR OTHER PURSE!" I dug through my closet and guess what I found? Yep! My ring! Now, mind you, this method doesn't always work this clearly and accurately, but lucky for me that day, it was bang on.

You too, can find a lost object like this. IF you meditate. IF you trust. If YOU want to use your powerful gifts for this plus so much more. The more you do fun and truly eye-opening exercises like this one, the more you will trust your gift, yourself and Spirit. Making it fun is key in the beginning of your journey. Fun is where it's at and it will allow you to be excited about what's coming next and slowly you will build up to the most amazing parts of your gifts.

Finding lost objects for yourself is one way. You may find that your friends begin to ask you to help them find their lost objects!

This is a good way to practice and see how your abilities work and improve. I have found lost glasses, lost wallet, an important piece of paper with lines and written in pencil. Sometimes I receive emails from people all over the world asking me to help find their very valuable objects.

A very distraught woman once emailed and asked me to help find her engagement ring. This was an interesting experience because this time, I used my clairvoyance to help locate it. Right away, I knew it was gone. Like *gone*, gone. But I asked Spirit and my team for help. Over the next few days, I was shown the story leading up to the moment it was gone. I saw clear visions of an argument with her husband, the room in which they argued, a safe, water and I kept hearing (clairaudience) "It's gone, it's gone." Unfortunately, for this woman who desperately wanted her ring back, we were unable to find it. Spirit did however clearly show us the exact events that led up to its disappearance. It is important to note that if the ring had been still intact and not gone, we would have seen its location.

1-800-Psychic

Before I tell you this, just get out of your head and forget everything you've ever heard or know about Psychics. Some Psychics are fakes and phonies and are out to take your money. Fortunately, the majority of Psychics are the real deal and their gifts are very real. So, here's the thing: You are a Psychic.

You don't don a Gypsy kerchief or hold a crystal ball. Thank God for that. You're a mom who probably frequents Starbucks and wipes their toddler's nose. Still a Psychic. Or a business woman who holds a very prestigious position and wears beautiful outfits free of stains. Psychic. Let be the one to tell you, YOU ARE A PSYCHIC. And that is a marvelous thing.

Psychics have a negative connotation attached to them or the word and that's why you may see the word, INTUITIVE, used more frequently. That word doesn't freak people out and it's gentler than Psychic. It's purely semantics. Doesn't matter what you call it. Your gifts are your gifts. Whether you hold a crystal ball or not.

Today, Intuitives and Mediums are becoming more and more accepted. That's because more and more people are waking up and having moments of "there has to be more to life than this" moments of clarity. Meditation groups, Reiki healing, and readings are gaining in popularity and thus becoming more mainstream. It is my hope that one day the word paranormal will actually become normal. We won't be afraid to come out of the spiritual closet. We will proudly use and share our gifts!

Hiding Your Gifts

Sadly, there are so many of you hiding in the above-mentioned Spiritual closet. Why are you doing that again? Oh, right. You're worried about what others will think of you. I get it. I did the same thing. I went through it. I hid it too when I resigned from my teaching position with the school board. I did it up until my last day of work. Streams of my co- workers came to say good-bye with well wishes and asked, "What are you going to do instead, again?" I stammered and hid. I made up stuff like how I was going into the Healing Arts (technically, Mediumship is a healing art) and that I would be opening my own spiritual biz. I may have told two people out of sixty that I was quitting to be a full-time Professional Medium. I worried what they thought. But then I made a choice. A really important choice.

I decided that it was more important that I come out of the closet to help and serve others than it was to dumb down my gifts and hide. Hiding didn't help anyone. Especially me. I knew it that day I stood in the classroom on the last day of school in June. The most powerful feeling came over me and that was the day

I decided teaching was no longer for me. Something way more powerful was guiding me to a brand-new path and nothing was going to stand in my way. Spirit and Source energy were in charge now. They were always in charge, I just didn't know it. All I had to do was follow the bread crumbs. But first I had to step out of my comfort zone and tell the world who I really was. That takes a lot of guts.

When I stopped hiding, so much good came out of it. Once I opened the door and stepped into my new life, I was welcomed with (mostly) open arms. The day I quit my job, I had *four* clients sign up for readings. That exact day! I guess the Big U approved of my decisions. ☺ I have helped so many people. I have done hundreds of readings. I get to make others feel better. How powerful and amazing is that? Can you do that from cowering in your closet? NO. You've got to get out of there now. It's not too late. People are going to say what they are going say. It's not important anyway. Who cares what they say? You are here to do this. You are here to share your gifts with the world.

You can decide. It's one day or day one. Are you going to step out of the spiritual closet and use your magic? Just decide that it's more important to use the gifts you have than it is to be afraid of what they think. Who gives a shit what they think? You are epic. You are incredible. You are here for a reason. You are needed in this world, and not just to help someone find their keys.

I Wanna See You Be Brave

Good segue way into this part of the chapter. Haven't you heard that song? I want to see you be brave. You don't need to quit your job, unless you don't like it and realize there is something bigger out there for you! Bravery comes in all forms. Maybe you start by telling someone you have your Reiki level one and they end up having a pain they need healed and you're just the healer to help. What if you don't tell anyone you can do Reiki? How are you supposed to help anyone if you keep that information to yourself? Yes, I may be on rant and it is your decision, but Reiki is effing cool and it helps others. And isn't that the reason we are all here? To help others.

I can't urge you enough to please stop hiding. Remember Harry Potter? What if he never came out from the closet under the stairs? There would be no Hagrid, Severus, or Dumbledore. We would always be Muggles. No School of Wizardry or Expecto Patronum. No magic. I'm actually tearing up here. Not only am I huge fan of all things Harry, I am a big fan of you sharing your magic too.

It takes balls to step it up and get out there. It's not easy and you are going to stumble and fall. I won't lie to you. I did it, too, and I fell on my face a bunch of times. I had messages in my inbox about how I wasn't "ready and should not be putting myself out there." How I was, "making the other Mediums look bad by being unexperienced." I didn't stop when I got that hate mail on the day of a sold-out event that said I was a fraud. I didn't quit when my first business *Reiki Moms* flopped and fizzled out, but I am never going to want to take it back. Not one single step of it. From the moment I decided to step into my bravery bad-assness, it's been the most amazing decision I've ever made. All it takes is a deep breath and a lot of courage.

I know you can do this.

You know that feeling that isn't coming from a place of fear. It's deeper. It's the strong inner knowing that something is meant for you or that you need to do something bigger than whatever it is you are currently doing. That's your Soul. That's Source. It's not ego. It's not fear-driven. It feels like excitement. It feels like passion. It feels joyful. There's a big difference between wanting to do something to help and serve others and actually going out there to do it. Your inner being (aka superpower) knows the right way. All you have to do is listen.

Stop ignoring the nudges. Once you decide, it's going to be the most amazing ride of your life.

Become a Medium (If You Want To!)

Becoming a Medium didn't happen overnight. If you had told me five years ago that I would quit a career with a pension to go out on my own as a Professional Medium, I would have called you crazy. It wasn't even on my radar. Nowhere in my mind did I think, "Man, it would be so cool to talk to dead people and make strangers cry!" Who would?

Attending an event with a Medium doing her thang was fate. As I sat in the audience anxiously awaiting a possible reading in the crowd, my entire body vibrated with excitement. I was in awe of how she delivered such profound and important message to those in attendance. How did she do that? How did she know what to say? Who was speaking to her? That moment changed my course forever. I had no idea then what was about to unfold, but I knew it was going to be life-changing.

And I wanted it bad after that. My inner being (superpowers) said it was time. Time? Time for what? Time to get to work. I took every course on Mediumship I could, read ten books on the subject, practiced my ass off, meditated constantly and was not going to let anyone or anything stop me. Except for the telling people part. I used to joke with my normal, non-spiritual work friends that where I was going was *classified.* There was no way I was telling them I was going to practice communicating with Spirits. What a weirdo.

But for reals. If this is something that is calling you, nudging you, seeing signs about, watching umpteen offers for Mediumship bombarding your social media news feed, there is something to be noticed. Better yet, have a reading done. You will be able to watch and experience how a Medium delivers this incredible gift.

I almost wrote job. Well, I did actually type the word job, but it didn't feel right so I deleted it and put in gift. To me, Mediumship isn't a job. It's a special and really important gift that we give to others. It helps them to heal and feel peace. And if you are a good Medium, your clients will completely believe you when you tell them their loved one in Spirit is still with them, every single day. They see what you've been doing (yes, everything!) They tell you important birthdays, names of your family members and friends, and so much more validating information. How amazing would that be to not only communicate with Spirit, but to change the lives of grieving families? That is why I say gift.

In the next and final (what??) chapter, we will talk about how life-changing this entire journey can be for you and others if you only step out into the world and show your gifts and superpowers off.

"You know that feeling that isn't coming from a place of fear. It's deeper. It's the strong inner knowing that something is meant for you or that you need to do something bigger than whatever it is you are currently doing. That's your Soul."

CHAPTER TEN

UNLEASH YOUR SUPERPOWERS

"Those who don't jump will never fly."
-Leena Ahmad-Almashat

Wear Your Cape Proudly

THE FIRST STEP in unleashing your super powerful gifts out into the world is *deciding* to unhide them. I know we talked about this in previous chapters and I can still feel some of you holding back. A gift can't be shared until you give it away.

That means deciding to be brave. Maybe you are already wearing and sharing There is much power in that for sure, but this is for the shy ones. The not-so-brave-ones who are worried about stepping out of that phone booth and revealing that big old "I" from under their coat. Truthfully, all it takes is a decision.

Once you see how powerful your intuition and you are, but you are hiding all the time, you may find yourself feeling super tired, not super powerful. Acknowledging you have a gift (or many) is the first step toward discovering a life beyond your wildest dreams. But getting out there and shining your light is the only way to this amazing place.

Now for those of you who ARE sharing and shining with your superpower and working to heal the world. What you are doing is more incredible and life-changing than you may realize. Not in an ego way, but a love way. Because what we do as Lightworkers, caregivers, Mediums, Reiki Practitioners, Angel Communicators has a profound effect on those we assist. By helping them realize their innate superpowers that they didn't know they had, they TOO, can find their capes and stand tall with them flapping in the wind.

When I decided to take the cape out, I felt a freedom I had never felt before. First the freedom came with leaving my soul-sucking career that I had outgrown. THEN even bigger feelings of joy, exhilaration, and happiness was the result of stepping out of the Spiritual closet and announcing to all who knew me that I was, in fact, ready to do amazing things. Things like: transform stranger's lives by bringing them peace out of turmoil and sadness, showing them that they were right when they felt like there was more to this life than what they could see. It's up to you what you do with your gift. The first step is saying, YES, I want to help, too.

So, hands on hips, all of you. Decide to wear your cape proudly. The hiding doesn't help anyone and that is what we all were chosen to do. It would be a disservice to not share. To not say, "How can I help/serve someone today?" The world needs a lot more of you. The world needs more of US.

No More GPS For You

Ready to use your intuition now for more than navigating your vehicle the correct route? YOU BETTER BELIEVE IT!

You wouldn't have come all the way to the last chapter of this book if you weren't meant to do just that.

OMG it's the last chapter of this book!! What?? I may need a minute to celebrate that! It's now December and an ungodly hour of 3:49 am and I sit here with my tea and cookies by the fireplace typing away. No one knows I'm awake or not in bed and the house is super quiet. I began writing this back in July and the word count is 29,142. There is snow on the ground. Back in the summer, I had no idea where this book would go or how long it would take me to finish. I just knew that when I didn't write, my inner superpowers were telling me to take it slow and that the right words would be written at the right time. I had to follow that feeling. That inner knowing sure is smart.

Now here I sit and am hoping that this chapter makes sense. It's in the wee hours of the morning, so I hope it's not gibberish and you can understand what I'm trying to teach you. My intuition is what woke me up and I felt like I needed to grab my laptop and start writing. I didn't know what words were going to come out onto the screen, but I trusted the nudge to get up. Doesn't matter that I have a client coming this morning for a reading. Time to write, Jen. Now I'm feeling like I'm just taking up pages, so I can finish this book and get it out to you.

I could go on all night telling you how I write this chapter, I can feel my Grandfather in Spirit watching me. I hear in my head (clairaudience) the song, "I always feel like, somebody's watching meeeeeee." I can see his outline in my mind (clairvoyance) and even his white bushy mustache. He's telling me to keep going (clairaudience) and that many people (you) are waiting for this dang book to get published. People are waiting to learn how to do what I'm doing right this second.

Author's note: I am now sitting on the porch of a condominium in Costa Rica (another manifestation that came true) writing this chapter. It has been 7 months since I have typed anything for this book. I was too afraid to share this book with you. I was too afraid you may not think it was good enough. I have told myself I am too busy. But the Universe keeps sending me signs. Someone just bought a copy of this unpublished book for her niece for her birthday. How do I not stand up and say NO MORE? I am doing this. I will finish this book and get it in your hands now. You guys needed this book and I am here to serve you. I am not afraid to share it now.

I know you have moments like this when you're awakened at 3 am as well and not just the times your newborn wakes up 1500 hundred times. Oh wait, that was me a few years ago. And maybe it's you too. If that's the case, how do you have time to read this book?? I didn't read for three years because I was always so busy with my four little kids. Or you don't have young kids any longer. You now have cats. Cats who stick their paw under the bathroom door now. Maybe you have a whole house of cats. In that case, you are a crazy cat lady. Two cats are cool. Speaking of cats, did you know that cats can see/hear/feel Spirits? That would mean, technically that cats have superpowers too. If your cat has abilities and is using them, WHY THE HECK AREN'T YOU?

AUTHOR'S NOTE: Cats are the best.

Summary of Steps

Time to take action, Jackson. Hey, I have a nephew named Jackson, but I spelled it wrong. He has an x in his name and Harry Potter glasses. I wonder if he knows he has superpowers? He's thirteen so he probably just wants to play on the iPad instead. Whoa, my intuition is telling me to stop dillydallying and get busy. Hi Jaxson!

Here is a summary of all the steps you need to take now to get this party started:

Step 1: New Kids on the Block song in my head now. Step by step. Ooh, baby. Gonna get to you gurlllll.

For Real Step 1:

Admitting I was right about you having inner powers. Whoops, I mean YOU were right. Because you knew this WHOLE time. You were born with it. Lying in the hospital bed with your new Mom, you knew. Why wouldn't you have it still? You've used it your whole life. Say to yourself: "I have a superpower and I am going to use it from now on!" You're going to use it be a Medium like me, find lost objects like your glasses that are on your head, make big decisions from now on no problem-o, know which direction you want your life to go into, whether or not to quit your own soul-sucking job or not. It's up to you. Use them. They're powerful.

Step 2: Trust.

Trust that shit. Seeing 111? Dude, why are you thinking negative thoughts right now? I hope you aren't thinking them about my book. 111 means keep your thoughts positive, remember? Angels, Spirit Guides, your Grandpa with the bushy mustache who is looking over your shoulder to make sure you don't check Facebook again till this chapter is done are all nudging you, guiding you and helping you every second of every day. Until you believe and trust that fact, you won't get very far.

Every day on my long commute to my old job, I would receive constant signs that it was time to quit. Moving trucks (hundreds of them), 555 (major life changes), 999 (a chapter is ending, for the love of God!) songs on the radio, stronger and stronger intuitive feelings. The list is so long. And it wasn't until I trusted Spirit and the Universe and that my intuition was on point, that I finally could see which way was up. If I hadn't trusted those signs, I wouldn't be here today at 4:21 am writing this to you. You'd be missing out on a really good book about intuition. I wonder how many times I wrote the word, "intuition" in this book. Probably a lot. I'm too tired to go count.

Step 3: Meditate

Meditate. You thought you were going to get out of meditating, didn't you? HA. No way. This step is probably the top three best things you can do to grow and strengthen your gifts. Wait. It IS the top three. Put down this book and meditate right now. Why not? Ohhhhhh because you love this chapter and want to hear more! Well, I don't want to disappoint you so...

Meditation is key. It is literally the key to connecting to Source energy. To opening your crown chakra and being who you truly are. Like, right now, I am connected to Source energy as I write this book. My intuition told me to be playful and have fun with it. It was feeling heavy and like a chore to write again but now as I sit here and type, I feel like Source has my back. I didn't meditate today but it's early and to be fair, I have been meditating every day for the past three years. That's how I can tune in and turn on the powers super quick. I'm connected. I'm tapped into where the magic is. You can't get there without quieting your mind. It's the only way.

Meditating is also a gift in itself. No really! I look forward to it. The minute I lay down and start to breathe deeply, everything goes away. The stress, the worry and lack mindset. Gone. I stop all resistance to what I'm manifesting as well when I'm quieting my mind. Things I want are coming quicker to me then. I feel peace and relaxation. I feel like the real me when I'm lying still and the thoughts come. Yes, you need to do the laundry and the dishes. But those can wait. Isn't getting quiet and hearing, feeling, sensing Source energy more important?

Do it. Do it now. The more you do, the more you will crave it, not dread it. And then, as you do, your gifts will explode, and flourish and you will be able to communicate with Spirit. How cool is that? Don't take my word for it. You got this. You'll thank me later.

Step 4: Believe

Believe that there IS more than nine-to-five, pay bills and die kind of semi-charmed kind of life. You don't need proof although there is plenty of that if you need it and just look around. The evidence is there. When you get to the point of believing is seeing and not the other way around, that's when the magic starts. Because the truth is, you are an extension of Source energy. As an Intuitive, Source energy works through you and isn't that a powerful truth to hear? That in of itself is incredible to learn, or to remember-since you came here with that knowledge within you and just "forgot".

You may not reach this believing stuff yet because we are all taught that we need big time evidence in order to believe in something. With practice, learning, and the eagerness to want to believe, eventually, it will all come rushing back to you with full force. This is where you can begin to manifest the life of your dreams, more money, more feelings of worthiness and possibilities, that perfect partner, and more. Believing is what tells the Universe that you trust that it has your back without the evidence to support it. You must have faith.

Step 5: Connection

Once you begin this wild and incredibly life-altering journey, you will feel more connected. To Spirit, to Source, and most importantly, to yourself. You cannot un-know what you now know. Know what I mean? Meditation alone provides the important connection. You will start to see how things really are. You may even start to question everything you've ever been taught and have believed your entire life. Your beliefs may start to shift and sway. You may find yourself wanting more. More information. More Mentors. More learning. More books. More, more, more. That's the connection at work.

You will also start to notice that you are craving more connection with like-minded (or as some like to say, like-hearted) people. How can you talk to your old bff about what you saw in meditation if she has no idea who Source is? Those old feelings of feeling "crazy" or like no one understands you will come up to the surface over and over. You may not want to share your new-found knowledge with anyone! A piece of advice: DO NOT KEEP IT TO YOURSELF! You are going to want validation and sharing what you now know with others who "get" you will be the most helpful thing you can do. Reaching out to various social media groups who will support and uplift you in your new journey will allow you to grow and develop your gifts. The idea is not to hide any longer in that closet, remember? You will be more likely to share your gifts and ideas with other "awake" souls.

Your connection to yourself will also change. You may eventually realize that you are a soul having a human experience and you have come to create. Daily meditation will strengthen that knowing. The more connected you are to Source energy, the more you will learn about yourself. Who you are and what you are here to do. And no, it's not to pay bills and die ☺ Trust me, it's a wild ride, but I guarantee you it is worth it. You have gifts that are meant to be shared so get out there and find your connections. Connections to others, Source, and yourself.

Spidey Senses on Steroids

Now that you've discovered and (hopefully) practiced your new-found gifts through meditation and finding Mentors you mesh with, things are going to get amped up. Your meditation game is strong, your connection to Source is soaring, and you've got your tribe who supports you on your spiritual journey.

What's next?

You may notice some cool things starting to happen now.

If you're open to it and are good at noticing, the following things are possible (and probable):

- Signs will literally be everywhere. Ask your Guides for signs and you will get them. Road signs, licence plates, repeating numbers, songs. All of it will be given to you in abundance. You just have to pay attention.
- Your meditations will change. You may start to see colours and images in your mind's eye and feel sensations as you connect. This is all normal and it just means you are connecting in a new and exciting way.
- You may find yourself buying every Spiritual book on the shelf. You want more information and understanding new concepts and ideas about Spirit are part of the gig. You will be a sponge; soaking everything you can up into your heart and mind.
- You will want to take courses on all things intuition, psychic abilities, and even Mediumship.
- You will begin to know things about other people without knowing why you know.
- You will get stronger feelings about the people you spend your time with the most and who you want to hang out with and who you do not. Trust these feelings as your intuition never lies.
- Predictions about outcomes for family and friends.
- Visions or thoughts that you feel are not your own. Again, trust it.
- Your creativity may go through the roof! Blogs, posts, book even may come out of "nowhere".

Take the Course Online

Speaking of courses…I happen to have one with the same name as this book! Coincidence? No such thing. This entire book came from one of those ideas that came "out of nowhere" one day a year ago as I was meditating. I was just sitting there in silence minding my own business. The idea behind *Unearth Your Intuition* is for all you still hiding in the Spiritual closet and you already know there is more to this life than what you can see with your eyes. There is more to life than day to day, little coincidences and just trudging along. I know the importance of connecting with yourself and Source and the powers that await each and every one of us and I want to share it with my students.

Unearth Your Intuition is broken down into thirty days and focuses on five of the steps needed to enhance and develop your abilities. The ones you thought you either didn't have at all or the ones you knew you did and are ready to use them to full capacity. All completed on Facebook (so there are no excuses why you can't participate) each week, my students are led through various exercises and challenges that allow them to step into their gifts. Learning how to meditate is the first step. Getting quiet allows for your connection with Source to grow and it is the only way to do this work. Yes, it is work but it is FUN work.

The next step after meditation is trust. Trust is a process. It will come with practice and evidence. We then move onto learning how to read Angel Cards for each other and ourselves. Angel Cards provide validation and confirmation to questions we may need guidance on. Manifesting, the Law of Attraction, and Clair's are the next and final steps of the program to complete. You also get to meet and support many other like-hearted individuals who are in the same boat as yourself. You are safe to learn in a supportive environment for the next thirty days. You will be inspired on a daily basis to challenge yourself, get out of your comfort zone and trust Spirit. You will be amazed just how often you are given signs and have never noticed before. Things you ask for will be delivered and magic abounds. Are you ready to unearth it? It's been there the whole time! You just need to find a way to discover how to navigate this incredible path that is now laid out right before your feet.

Your Life Will Never Be the Same

Why would you want it to be the same? Like I said, you can't unknow what you now know. It's impossible. Let me assure you, you won't want to go back to normal. You may have moments where you think you are off your rocker and people think you've gone mad, but trust me, you are the one who is right. You are the one with all the power now that you've opened your eyes and your intuition. You are the one who said yes and will now have the incredible power to create anything you wish. Once you know, you know.

When you learn how to manifest using the Law of Attraction, you will be able to create the life you always wanted because there is nothing you cannot be, do, or have. When you learn to trust the signs and symbols that Spirit is sending, you will be able to make decisions quicker and make better choices for yourself. You will stop saying yes when you want to say no. You will realize how powerful you are and that you have incredible gifts that are meant to be used. Your new life is waiting. All you need to do is start.

Remember no matter what you decide to do next, your gifts can help others as well. From locating lost items such as rings or important papers to providing them with messages from their loved ones in Spirit, you are here to serve in any way you can. That is why I wrote this book. For you. To help you discover your gifts and get you prepared to use them. This book can be your starting guide to show you what your next step is.

There is so much waiting for you now and when find the courage, I hope you dance. Wait. What? That's a song. I mean, I hope you shout it from the rooftop: "I HAVE SUPERPOWERS AND I AM GOING TO USE THEM FROM NOW ON! NO MORE HIDING OR CARING WHAT THEY THINK!" Not caring what others think of you or your gifts is a gift itself. And who doesn't love gifts? Presents. When it's **not** your birthday. Surprise gifts like chocolate.

Now I want chocolate. And cake.

Have fun with your new-found gifts and enjoy your new relationship with Spirit. It'll be the best thing you have ever done for you. It's your time. Get out there and show them who's boss. I mean, who's the best. I mean, show them your secret "s" you've been hiding under your clothes in the closet with that scar on your forehead. It is time.

Oh crap.

The end.

ARE YOU READY TO UNEARTH AND UPLEVEL YOUR INTUITION

IN JUST 30-DAYS?

OH MY GOSH, I KNOW YOU!! You are like me before I knew! The one who believes they are alone in their "odd" and "unexplainable" experiences. You feel like you just may be going crazy or "losing it". The feather you discovered on your shoe when it's the most blustery day of the year. The repeating numbers on the clock that you just "happen" to notice at exactly 11:11. Does this sound like you? Have no fear! Your superpowers are here!

Aaaaand I totally see you. Nervously biting your nails and looking the other way when you see a license plate that says, LOVEPAPA or GO4IT. You're doubting and chalking it up to "coincidence" even when you repeatedly notice signs all around you.

If you're one of these amazingly awesome "kindabelievers", then this is for you. I feel you. I used to BE you. There are MORE of you then you realize. It's like we've all crammed into this invisible "Spiritual" closet and we are all afraid to open the door to the Spirit World! But if you look around you, there are a lot of you crammed in the closet. You aren't alone in this! There is SO much information and magic available to you if you just choose to open the door. You can step outside of the dusty, stuffy and normal, crampin' your style tiny room and not only be SHOWN all of the incredible, exciting world of Spirit and the Universe, but LEARN how to navigate in it.

Don't believe me yet? Thinking, "Pffft! I Love MY cozy closet where it's all safe and stuff." Once you decide to open the door and step into your BEST life, things will dramatically change for you. What you doubted before and shied away from due to doubt, will magically appear.

Here's what I'm talkin' about:

- When you open up to the Universe and all it has to offer you, you will begin a super- quieting of your mind lifestyle. Establishing a concrete meditation practice in your life will ENHANCE it beyond your wildest imagination. You will become more YOU-ER than YOU've ever been before. Your truest, most authentic YOU. How freaking powerful is THAT?
- Once you have the meditating feels, you can begin to TAP into Source. You will find the confidence to rock the new-found relationship with Spirit and all it has to offer you. PS it's been there the WHOLE time!! You just didn't notice!
- Building a new relationship is a two-way street. You will learn the secret formula to building a super-tight and trusting relationship between you and Spirit. SO much so that you won't be afraid to ASK for material objects! Not only that, but Spirit WILL deliver the goods. All you gotta do is TRUST.
- Trusting the insight, clarity and signs is all part of the deal. Once the Universe delivers and shows you how massively giving it can be, you won't ever wanna stop! Breaking up is not an option once you open up to it!
- Learn how to make the Law of Attraction work for you. Your mind, beliefs and thoughts create your exact life you

are experiencing right now! Want something different, you can co-create a new reality by tapping straight into Source energy.

YOU ARE SO WORTH IT.

- You will leave with the air-tight inner knowing that Spirit is all around you, supporting you times infinity.
- Transformation is not only a possibility but WILL occur. Go from ho hum to HOLY INTUITION, BATMAN. Superpowers. Bam.
- You will no longer be the same person you were before you began this journey. You won't be able to hide your super powers any longer because your eyes and your mind will be blown WIDE open. The possibilities of what you choose after we are done working together will be endless. Limitless.
- You will have the tools to manifest tangible objects into your being. The miracles await.
- You will no longer need to seek outside assistance because you will have the power and gift to FEEL and INTUIT your life all on your very own! No more 1-888-PSYCHIC for you!
- Imagine a world where you can FEEL your way through your day-today decisions without freaking out. Let your inner GPS guide you with ease! Listening to those nudges will be easier to follow. Especially when you are going the wrong way on a road trip. ;)
- Understanding when the Angels and your Team have important messages for you. When you see 111 and 555, you will have no doubt what it means. None. That's how badass at this you will be.

Want to try this course on for size? Let's start RIGHT NOW. Here is an awesome challenge for you to try out and give you a taste of what's to come when you say YES to Spirit and bust out of the dusty, over crowded closet.

I want you to close your eyes and just feel. Sit in that chair and do not move. Quiet your mind for a sec and in your head, I want you to ask Spirit for a sign. It can be a song that has a message for you, a number combo, or my personal fave, a feather. Then let it go. When you get it, you are ready to sign up for this program!

$99 for 30-days www.mediumjenabra.com

ABOUT THE AUTHOR

JENNIFER CURRENTLY LIVES in Shelburne, Ontario Canada with her four kids, her amazing husband, Chad and their two cats. After teaching small children to write their name and tie their shoes for over a decade, Jennifer is now pursuing a more spiritual path and career. She is a Professional Medium, Spiritual Mentor and now a published author on the topic of intuition.

With her kids being much older now and having the support of her husband, Jennifer is now a world traveler. After visiting places such as New Orleans and Costa Rica, she is finding her way to more adventures as she intuitively chooses them.

With this book, Jennifer has shared her own inner knowing and spiritually guided information with her readers, so that they too, may find their path and purpose.

Jennifer is thrilled to have finished her first book and is ready to write her second one, maybe in Bali.